ALL-TERRAIN
PUSHCHAIR WALKS
Cheshire

Norman Buckley

SIGMA
Leisure

Published by Sigma Leisure – an imprint of
Sigma Press, Stobart House, Pontyclerc, Penybanc Road,
Ammanford, Carmarthenshire SA18 3HP.

British Library Cataloguing in Publication Data
A CIP record for this book is available from the British Library.

ISBN: 978-1-85058-844-3

Typesetting and Design by: Sigma Press, Ammanford, Carms

Cover photograph: Cheshire countryside *(Simon C. Buckley)*

Maps: Bute Cartographics.

Photographs: Norman Buckley, except where noted.

Printed by: Bell & Bain Ltd, Glasgow

Disclaimer: the information in this book is given in good faith and is believed to be correct at the time of publication. No responsibility is accepted by either the author or publisher for errors or omissions, or for any loss or injury howsoever caused. Only you can judge your own fitness, competence and experience. Do not rely solely on sketch maps for navigation; we strongly recommend the use of appropriate Ordnance Survey (or equivalent) maps.

Preface

The successful expansion of the All Terrain Pushchair series of walking books into many parts of Britain is entirely consistent with the present-day objective of facilitating maximum possible public access to the countryside. Parents (and grandparents!) can now set out with very young children to follow the carefully chosen and assessed walking routes in these books, confidant that the chances of meeting with some insurmountable obstacle such as a high stile or impassable gate are minimal and that other factors possibly affecting the use of an ATP such as steep slopes and excessive mud will be evaluated and mentioned in the text.

The popularity of the ATP, coupled with the use of an ATP Walks book, brings large areas of lovely countryside within easy reach, with the double benefit of allowing adults to discover or rediscover that countryside, whilst at the same time making an early introduction to these wonderful places for young children.

Norman Buckley

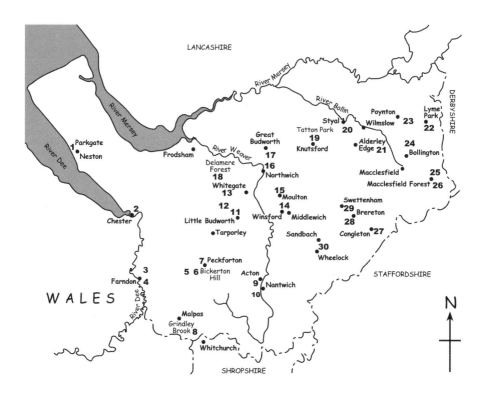

Locations of Walks

Contents

Introduction

This book contains thirty recommended walking routes, many with possible variations, some circular and some out and back, ranging from 1.5km (1 mile) to 6.5km (4 miles) in length. The maximum total ascent in any case is no more than 150m (492ft). The great majority have much less ascent. They are set out on the location plan preceding the contents pages. In making this selection from the large number of walking routes available throughout the sizeable county of Cheshire, assumptions have been made.

The first assumption is that even strong and experienced country walkers will be looking for shorter walks when pushing an ATP. The normal needs of a baby or young child will likewise militate against long excursions. The second assumption is that, even within the limits imposed by an ATP, walkers will expect as great a diversity of route and scenery as can be achieved. Accordingly, although these walks are predominantly short, they do cover the whole county, including the hill country of the east.

Routes and Grades

Each walk has an introductory section, with succinct information on distance, total ascent, start/parking place, relevant Ordnance Survey map and refreshments. This is followed by a description of the area, mentioning features likely to be of interest to the walker.

Most important is the 'assessment' of the route relative to the use of an ATP, on a scale of 1 to 5. This grade represents a summation of the likely difficulties. Inevitably, this grading carries a risk of over simplification of a possibly complex situation and of subjectivity, but it does have the advantage of facilitating a speedy decision on the suitability or otherwise of a proposed walk. As a general guide, Grade 1 is applied to a short walk along a route with little ascent, without awkward stiles, tight kissing gates or flights of steps and with reasonable surfaces underfoot, without serious mud. A typical example would be a walk predominantly along a canal towpath or the trackbed of a disused railway line. At the other extreme, a Grade 5 includes hard work for the pusher(s) of the ATP; the walk may be longer, say 5 or 6 miles and/or there may be steep or prolonged ascents, with awkward gates, stiles or steps. The walking surface could well include mud, rock or uneven paving. The more difficult routes really require two adults to manage the ATP. Most walks fall between these extremes, with the features which result in the grading being mentioned in each case.

The route of the walk is then described fully, with an accompanying sketch plan.

All Terrain Pushchairs

ATPs have become increasingly popular during the past few years, their rugged build quality ensuring durability and a 'go anywhere' capability which justifies their higher cost. Inevitably, they are heavier than more flimsy pushchairs but the large wheels with pneumatic tyres ensure that they are easy to push and to manoeuvre, as anyone who has encountered them in supermarkets will realise. There are several makes available, all with a wide range of accessories. First time buyers should decide on their priorities and then examine several different models. A three wheel format (often with the front wheel doubled) is usual, with large (about 30cm, 12") wheels with pneumatic tyres, quick release system for the wheels, easy folding for carrying in a car boot, comprehensive weather protection for summer and winter and a good braking system. Variables

An example of a modern ATP

include the unloaded weight of the ATP, its size, open and folded, one or two child capacity, lockable swivel or fixed front wheel(s), adapters for carrying very young babies, suspension, and extra insulation for the feet. All should have a hand pump for tyre inflation and a puncture repair kit. A trial with passenger is highly desirable, although the floor of a showroom can hardly replicate some of the conditions found along the routes in this book!

Weather Protection

Parents will hardly need reminding that, even in warm weather, children immobile in push chairs need much more warm cover than the adults who are working hard to push an ATP, possibly uphill. Don't forget hands and toes!

Adult Wear

Basically, the requirements are the same as for walking without an ATP. For the easier walks, trainers or similar will suffice in most cases, although it must be said that large rocks, loose smaller stones, uneven paving, tree roots and clinging mud will all be encountered. Experienced walkers, at least those of the older generation, will regard traditional walking boots, with rigid moulded soles, as essential in these circumstances. Other than during exceptional spells of reliably dry weather, waterproof outer garments should always be taken on a walking expedition.

Precautions

The walks in this book are generally short and, without a pushchair or young children, would be undemanding, not needing the sound advice which is normally given to those who are undertaking mountain ascents and treks across remote areas. However, even in the relatively gentle Cheshire countryside, it is wise to be a little over-cautious when accompanied by young children:

☆ Check the weather forecast. Being caught in sudden thunderstorms, snow blizzards or heavy rain is, at best, thoroughly unpleasant and possibly frightening for children and could, at worst, be dangerous.

☆ Carry a mobile 'phone (there may be areas without a signal, particularly in the hill country).

☆ Carry a basic first-aid kit.

☆ Always have water or other cold drink (not fizzy) available.

☆ Carry some high-energy food both for adults and children.

☆ Don't be too ambitious; walk well within your capabilities.

☆ Allow more time than you expect to need.

Cheshire

The reputation of Cheshire as a great dairy farming county, large swathes of rich farming land grazed by herds of cud-chewing, contented cows, fails to recognise its considerable diversity. The hill country to the east of the county, the fringe of the Peak District National Park, including peaks such as Shutlingsloe and the great expanses of Lyme Park and Macclesfield Forest, are commonly and erroneously regarded as part of Derbyshire. As might be expected, this area includes some of the most interesting and challenging walking routes. Likewise, the long ridge of sandstone, which extends from Frodsham in the north to the Shropshire border near Whitchurch, adds to the overall diversity. The designated Sandstone Trail is only one of the many possibilities for interesting walks on this comparatively high ground.

Even the flatter part of Cheshire is pleasantly varied. The northern fringe reaches into the outer suburbs of Manchester and to the valley of the River Mersey, whilst to the west are the River Dee and the Welsh border, not far from the foothills of the mountains, and the Wirral peninsula. The county is criss-crossed by railways and canals, several of the former now disused, providing attractive designated routes for walkers and others. The towpaths of the canals, many passing through unspoilt countryside, are likewise much used by walkers. Several stately homes are surrounded by extensive and attractive parkland, accessible by the general public. All these provide opportunities that are ideal for use with an ATP.

Maps and Sketch Maps

The route directions and sketch maps are sufficient for following any of the walks in this book. However, for many people the enjoyment of a walk is enhanced by the use of a large-scale map. The Ordnance Survey Explorer series, at a scale of 1:25,000, is excellent, having a wealth of detail. Sheets 257, 266, 267, 268, OL 1 (a little), OL 24 (very little) all include part of Cheshire. Use of the 1:50,000 Landranger series is more economical, but at the smaller scale there is obviously less detail. Relevant sheets are 109, 117,118.

Numbers on the sketch maps all cross-reference with instructions in the text. Start/finish points are denoted thus (s).

Walk 1: Parkgate and the Wirral Way

Assessment: *Grade 2.*

An easy level walk combining the estuary-side road at Parkgate with a section of the trackbed of a former railway line, now designated as the Wirral Way. Grade 2 only because of the descent of a flight of steps.

Distance: 4km (2½ miles)

Total ascent: Negligible.

Start/car parking: Free car park at the end of a cul-de-sac which leaves the Parkgate estuary-side road at the north end of the village, grid reference 274790.

Refreshments: Inns at either end of the estuary-side road. Coffee shop and ice cream parlour.

Map: Ordnance Survey Explorer 266, Wirral and Chester, 1:25,000.

The Area

Despite the proximity of Liverpool and Birkenhead, the Wirral peninsula has interesting walks, not least by the side of the estuary of the River Dee and along the trackbed of the former railway line which connected Hooton with West Kirby. Before the changes to local government boundaries in 1974, the whole of the Wirral was in Cheshire. Now much of the area is included in Merseyside although the present route just stays within the Cheshire boundary.

Several hundred years ago there were busy ports along the north-east side of the Dee estuary and at Chester. As progressive silting made access to Chester increasingly difficult in the 16th and 17th centuries, a new quay was constructed at Parkgate, ten miles downstream. However, despite attempts at dredging, the silting of the estuary continued, with the consequent moving of the shipping to Liverpool and the neighbouring estuary of the River Mersey. The

Parkgate saltmarsh and village *(Photograph: Anthony Annakin-Smith)*

Flintshire hills are now seen from Parkgate across a broad expanse of mud, sand and shallow water, rich in coastal bird life.

The railway from Hooton to Parkgate was opened in 1866, the continuation to West Kirby following in 1886. The line was single track only throughout its life although all the bridges were built to accommodate a possible future doubling which never happened. The predominantly flat countryside meant that gradients are easy and engineering works are minimal. After closure in 1962, the relevant local authorities spent a great deal of money in developing the trackbed as a route for walking, cycling and horse riding, a major component of the Wirral Country Park, with a visitor centre at Thurstaston. As is usual on disused former railway lines, the wildlife is rich and varied.

The Walk

From the far end of the car park, head along a tarmac path to a gate on

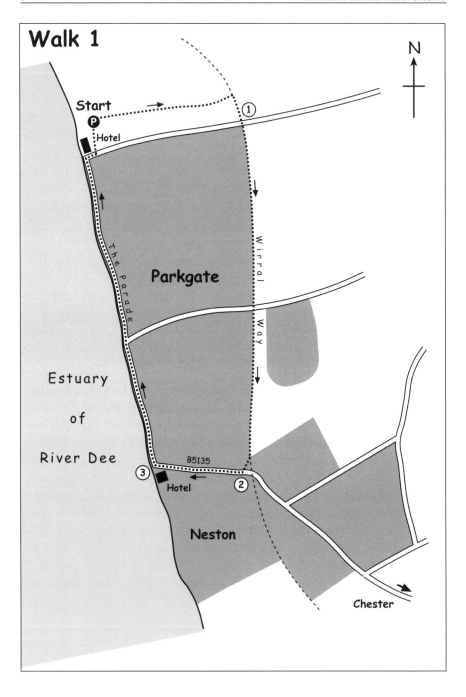

the right in 30m. There is a 'Wirral Way' signpost. Go through the gate and follow a lane, rising gently. Reach a bridge over the former railway line, designated the 'Wirral Way'.

1. Cross the bridge and turn right at a 'Wirral Way' signpost to descend a flight of about 20 steps to the trackbed. Turn left to continue along the Way, with a choice between the main track and a lesser track at the top edge of the cutting. Pass under a road bridge, the surface becoming concrete as the Way remains in a shallow cutting. Cross a bridge over a lane. A descending ramp here provides a short way back to the car park if required. Continue to a point where the tracks apparently fork, at the site of the former Parkgate station. Fork right, along a cobbled path. At a residential road turn left, to join the main road in 20m. There is a static exhibit of a truck on rails.

2. Turn right to head for the estuary along the roadside pavement. Note the old World War II 'pill box' on the bank opposite and an entrance to a further part of the Wirral Country Park.

3. Reach the side of the estuary at the Old Quay Inn. Turn right to walk along the roadside pavement, a fine promenade, passing a coffee shop and an ice cream parlour, enjoying the splendid views across the estuary and the abundant bird life. Turn left at the inn at the far end of the promenade to return to the car park.

Walk 2: Chester City Walls

Assessment: Grade 3

An unusual route for this book within the city of Chester, entirely achievable with an ATP and with a wealth of interest. A fair number of steps to be negotiated. As the walls are very popular with visitors, it might be advisable to avoid Bank Holidays and other peak times.

Distance: 3km (2 miles).

Total ascent: Negligible, apart from several flights of steps.

Start/car parking: Pay and display car park, with public conveniences, entered close to the city end of Grosvenor Bridge, grid reference 657404.

Refreshments: Hut at car park entrance. Numerous cafés and restaurants close to wall access points.

Map: Ordnance Survey Explorer 266, Wirral and Chester, 1:25,000.

The Area

The fine city of Chester is packed with historic and present day interest. Visitors will benefit from the use of a guide book and/or leaflets obtainable from the Tourist Information Centre.

Walking round the walls provides a panoramic view of much of the city, ancient and modern, including the famous Eastgate clock that was erected to celebrate Queen Victoria's Diamond Jubilee in 1897. From the walls thera are views of the River Dee, the Shropshire Union Canal, the racecourse and longer views to the Welsh hills.

The Eastgate clock: icon of Chester

The Walk

Leave the car park at the river end, walking by the riverside past County Hall, as far as Lower Bridge Street, which is crossed by the Wall (Bridgegate).

1. Turn left to go under the Wall, then immediately right to rise along a gentle ramp beside the wall, soon reaching the walkway along the top. The weir across the river is impressive; modern apartments on the far bank are rather less so. As the Wall bears left, away from the river do not go up the steps towards Eastgate. Keep left at the lower level, rising steadily to Park Street. Rake back sharp right up a ramp to regain the top of the Wall, turning left to continue. Public gardens below to the right contain Roman remains, including a hypocaust. The amphitheatre is a short distance further to the right.

2. Ascend a flight of steps to cross the bridge over Newgate. Continue past a level connecting pathway which leads into the Grosvenor shopping precinct. Steps up to the right lead to the bridge over Eastgate, with its splendid clock. The cathedral now dominates the view to the left; pass King Charles' Tower as the Wall bends to the left, with the canal now in its deep cutting below to the right. Go up and down steps to cross Northgate on another bridge. Pass Morgan's Mount watchtower, then cross a modern bridge over a dual carriageway road. The views into Wales are now extensive. Descend a long flight of steps, pass Pemberton's Parlour, the remains of a medieval round tower, and cross the railway line to reach Boldwaldesthorne's Tower, at the north-west corner of the Walls. Until the 13th century, the River Dee lapped against the base of this tower, which protected the port below. From the 14th century, the river changed course so in 1323 the Water Tower was built at the far end of a spur wall to protect the adjacent quays.

3. Bear left, cross the railway line again, descending gently to road level. Fork right to stay on top of the Wall. Go up a few steps to cross the bridge over Watergate and continue along the roadside

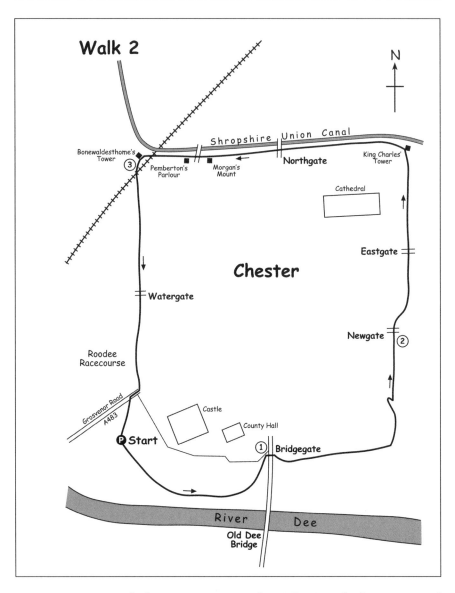

Walk 2

N

Shropshire Union Canal

Bonewaldesthome's
Tower
③
Pemberton's
Parlour

Morgan's
Mount

Northgate

King Charles'
Tower

Cathedral

Eastgate

↓

Watergate

Chester

Newgate
②

Roodee
Racecourse

Grosvenor Road
A483

Castle

County Hall

🅿 Start

① Bridgegate

River   Dee

Old Dee
Bridge

pavement, with the race course to the right. Reach the main road
close to the end of Grosvenor Bridge. Cross over to the car park,
either down steps at the near end or by walking down the adjacent road to the vehicular entrance at the river end.

Walk 3: Farndon and the River Dee

Assessment: *Grade 4*

The route necessitates the negotiation of three stiles, all of which are comparatively low, a grass path and probably a fair amount of mud at Crewe Hall Farm.

Distance: 5.5km (3½ miles)

Total ascent: 20m (66ft).

Start/car parking: Large informal riverside parking area in Farndon, accessed by a ramp descending to the left from the main road immediately before the traffic lights at the end of the bridge over the river, grid reference 413544.

Refreshments: Inns in Farndon.

Map: Ordnance Survey Explorer 257, Crewe and Nantwich, 1:25,000.

The Area

Farndon is a pleasant little Dee-side town, facing the Welsh town of Holt across the River Dee, very much a frontier. During the Civil War, this frontier was of some importance as the Parliamentarian forces needed to cross into Wales in order to cut off supply routes to Chester Castle, which was garrisoned for the King. Holt Bridge was guarded but, with the aid of a distractionary manoeuvre, the Parliamentarian troops forced a crossing. Farndon has traditional timber-framed black-and-white buildings, a few shops and the parish church of St Chad's.

Holt Bridge is of great antiquity; a former toll house stood in the middle, but by the 18th century this had been demolished. Holt also has the ruins of a medieval Border castle.

The Walk

Walk to the far end of the parking area and continue along a good track, forking right on a board walk in 50m, staying close to the river. To the left in this area is the Dee Cliff, a low sandstone outcrop.

1. At a junction with a seat leave the made-up track, following the riverside path to the right, over a mixture of earth and grass. Cross over a tributary stream. Across the river is Holt church. Negotiate the first stile; the ruins of Holt Castle are now in view across the lazy-flowing Dee. Negotiate the second (waymarked) stile before passing under the bridge carrying the main by-pass road across the river. Negotiate the third stile, go straight ahead at a junction; the path is now rather rough.

2. At a junction close to the river bank, turn left along a path at the edge of a field. There are waymarks, including 'Marches Way' and a redundant stile at the junction. Continue along a grassy lane, soon rising quite steeply to pass Crewe Hall Farm, the track likely to be muddy from the passage of farm vehicles. Reach a surfaced road

3. Turn left to follow the road past the entrance to Crewe Hall Farm, bending to the right to join a more major road. Turn left, to walk along the road for 300m, passing a terrace of cottages.

4. Turn left immediately after the cottages, into Crewe Lane South, passing through most of Crewe hamlet, including a tiny Primitive Methodist chapel. Pass Meadow View Farm before reaching the end of the road close to the main by-pass road, A534. Go through a small gate on the right, descend to cross the road, then rise along a track on the opposite side to a gate followed by bollards. Continue along a road into the fringe of Farndon. Pass two residential roads on the left (Meadow Close and Orchard Grove).

5. Turn left at Quarry Hill to follow the roadside footpath to the far end. At the end of the road continue along a surfaced footpath for 50m. Turn right at the end, reaching a road in less than 100m.

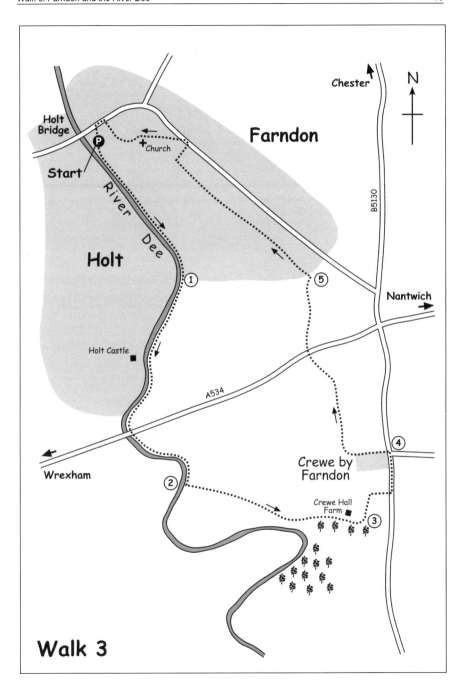

Walk 3

There is an attractive timber-framed house opposite. Turn left at the road to head towards the church. Pass a small car parking area and the Parish Church of St Chad, steadily downhill. Cross a little road and continue down a track opposite,

Timber-framed house at Farndon

soon reaching the main road. Turn left towards Holt Bridge and then left again in 40m to return to the car parking area, passing the public conveniences.

Walk 4: Farndon – shorter walk

Assessment: Grade 1.

An easy little walk combining riverside track with Farndon village.

Distance: 2km (1¼ miles).

Total ascent: Very little, less than 10m (33ft).

Start/car parking: As for walk 3.

Refreshments: As for walk 3.

Map: Ordnance Survey Explorer 257, Crewe and Nantwich, 1:25,000.

The Area

As for walk 3.

The River Dee at Farndon

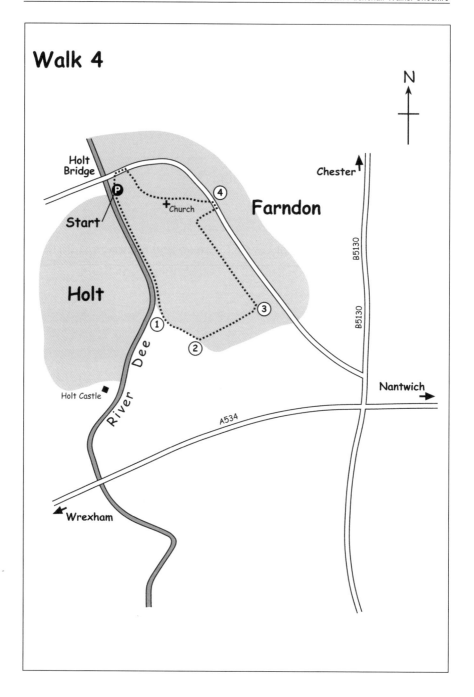

The Walk

Start along the same track as for the longer Farndon walk.

1. At point 1 of that route keep left along the made-up track.

2. At the end of that track go through a gap in the hedge ahead and turn left to follow a broad lane between hedges, rising gently. Ignore all paths to the right, ascending steadily but without difficulty. Enter the Farndon built-up area, reaching tarmac at Quarry Hill.

3. Turn left along the roadside footpath. At the far end of this residential road, continue along a surfaced footpath for 50m. At the end of the path turn right, reaching a road in less than 100m. There is an attractive timber-framed house opposite.

4. Turn left to head for the church. Pass a small parking area and then the parish church of St Chad, going steadily downhill. Cross a little road and continue down the track opposite to reach the main road. Turn left, towards Holt Bridge, and then left again to return to the car park down the access ramp.

Walk 5: Maiden Castle

Assessment: Grade 5.

The route includes some quite steep ascent and lengths of narrow track, some rough-surfaced.

Distance: 4.5km (2¾ miles).

Total ascent: 115m (377ft).

Start/car parking: Small informal National Trust car park at the south-west edge of Bickerton Hill. Accessed by the 'Coach Road', which leaves the A534 to the south from close to Barnhill. In less than 1½ miles turn left along a minor cul-de-sac lane heading straight for the woodland of Bickerton Hill. The car park is at the end of the road, in less than a quarter of a mile, grid reference 494525.

Refreshments: None en route.

Map: Ordnance Survey Explorer 257, Crewe and Nantwich, 1:25,000.

The Area

Bickerton Hill rises steeply from the adjacent agricultural land, a striking part of the long sandstone ridge which rune from north to south across west Cheshire. Crowning the hill is Maiden Castle, an Iron Age earthwork with banks and excavations still evident. Formerly a substantial area of wild heathland, the hill now has a fair amount of encroachment, mainly woodland. The sides of the hill on the north and west are particularly steep, with tracks not recommended for ATPs. The views from the top are excellent, extending for many miles on a clear day.

The Walk

Walk down the access road for a few metres and turn left at a 'National Trust. Bickerton Hill' 'Sandstone Trail' sign. Rise at once, initially on tarmac.

1. In 100m turn right at a Sandstone Trail signpost for 'Willeymoor and Whitchurch'. In a few metres there is an awkward left kink in the track which can be avoided by going behind the signpost and ascending a path across the grass, soon rejoining the Trail. Continue on a generally good track along the bottom fringe of Hether Wood, passing occasional waymarks and the foot of a flight of log steps. Pass a National Trust sign.

2. Immediately before the track begins to descend, fork left, soon rising quite steeply through woodland on a path which has stones and rough patches; this is the most difficult part of the walk. Reach a house with extensive outbuildings. Turn right here to follow a broad level forestry road for almost 400m. At a junction, turn left to pass a waymarked gate in 40m then rise along another forestry road, initially flanked by trees but soon becoming an open track across heathland.

3. Reach a junction of paths at Maiden Castle, with information board on a sandstone block. Before commencing the return, a short ascent to the right leads to the summit of the castle in a few

The remains of Maiden Castle *(Photograph: Graham Beech)*

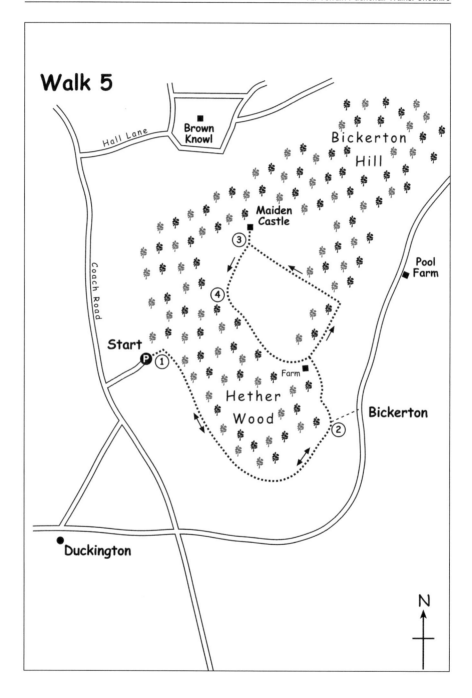

metres and is recommended, both for observing the earthworks and for the splendid views to north, west and south. Return to point 3. The return starts by turning left from the approach path (straight ahead if returning from the castle top) along a well-used easy track descending gently to a waymarked gate.

4. Bear left to another (locked) gate with an awkward kissing gate beside in a few metres. Go through (over?) and continue along a grass path with the fence on the left. At the far corner, follow the waymark round to the left, staying close to the fence to approach the house and outbuildings passed on the outward route. Go through a farm gate on the left to pass the buildings and reach the junction to rejoin the outward route. Turn right to descend the narrow path and return to the car park.

Walk 6: Bickerton Hill

Assessment: Grade 4.

A short walk but with two tight kissing gates, at least one of which requires lifting of an ATP, plus a fair amount of ascent.

Distance: 2.5km (1½ miles).

Total ascent: 85m (279ft).

Start/car parking: National Trust car park in (unsurfaced) Pool Lane, grid reference 503530, accessed from the minor road which leads from Bickerton Church to Duckington. Leave this road by a small pond, almost opposite Pool Farm,

Refreshments: None en route.

Map: Ordnance Survey Explorer 257, Crewe and Nantwich, 1:25,000.

The Area

This is an attractive circuit, following the Sandstone Trail around the northern part of Bickerton Hill, formerly an area of upland heath, now largely wooded. At the highest point (903m – 633ft,) is a memorial, from which there are extensive views to north and west. The return uses a short length of a very minor public road.

The Walk

Leave the car park through the tree stump bollards, to a gate in 30m. Continue uphill on a wide, sandy, track. Bear right at a fork to reach a 'Sandstone Trail' signpost in a further 100m.

1. Turn right, rising more steeply on a similar track, reaching another signpost in 100m. Turn left for 'Rawhead and Beeston', rising over some rough sandstone before walking along the top of the scarp. The extensive views include Brown Knowl village, below, and Peckforton Hill to the north-east. At the highest

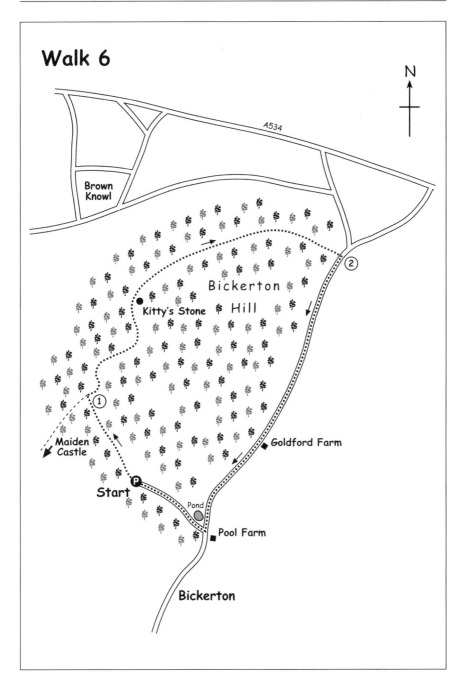

Walk 6

N

A534

Brown
Knowl

Bickerton
Hill

Kitty's Stone

②

Maiden
Castle

①

Goldford Farm

Start

P

Pond

Pool Farm

Bickerton

Bickerton Hill

point is the 'Kitty's Stone' memorial. The track soon begins to descend through woodland, with a few obstructive tree roots. Pass a mini sandstone cliff, undercut to form a shallow cave. There are occasional waymarks. As the trail descends a flight of steps, a short diversion to the right is better for ATPs, rejoining the wide path at the bottom of the flight. The track continues to weave its way through the woodland, steadily downhill, reaching an awkward kissing gate. There is now meadow to the left and then another awkward kissing gate. (ATPs can probably be pushed under the adjacent fence).

2.   Reach the public road, a very minor lane, turning right to walk by the roadside for half a mile, passing Goldford Farm before reaching the junction by the little pond. Turn right to walk up Pool Lane to the car park.

Walk 7: Peckforton and Higher Burwardsley

Assessment: *Grade 4.*

A relatively long walk with demanding ascents. Two awkward kissing gates. Good surfaces throughout.

Distance: 6.5km (4 miles).

Total ascent: 115m (377ft)

Start/car parking: small free car park under trees by the Peckforton village institute, grid reference 538566.

Refreshments: Pheasant Inn at Higher Burwardsley.

Map: Ordnance Survey Explorer 257, Crewe and Nantwich, 1:25,000.

The Area

Peckforton and Higher Burwardsley are both rather scattered little settlements, one on each side of the great steep-sided sandstone mass of Peckforton Hill which forms part of the long ridge which runs north to south across west Cheshire. The hill is largely wooded; at the north eastern end the 19th century Peckforton Castle is now a hotel. Most of the hill top is owned by the Peckforton Estate and is used for off-road driving training. The Cheshire Workshops Craft Centre at Higher Burwardsley is a considerable visitor attraction, with restaurant and children's play facilities. The route of this walk crosses the hill at a low point, with moderate gradients, returning along part of the designated Sandstone Trail around the north-eastern end. The final mile is along Stone House Lane, a quiet road.

The Walk

Leave the car park along the access roadway (there is a short cut to Hill Lane, but it includes a flight of steps). Turn left at the public road, Stone House Lane.

Gatehouse to Peckforton Hotel, former castle

1. Turn left again in a few metres into Hill Lane to commence the long ascent, on tarmac, towards Peckforton Hill. Pass a pile of great sandstone boulders on the left before reaching a junction. Go straight ahead, now on an old cobbled surface, soon passing a vehicular barrier and then under a neat stone bridge. Ignore any tracks to left or right. The gradient eases and an open area to the right, Waste Hill, is passed. There is an overgrown small pond on the right. Pass farm buildings, now descending gently on tarmac. Pass a leaning stone pillar and a kissing gate ('Sandstone Trail') on the left, heading for 'Pheasant Inn' and 'Beeston'.

2. In less than 100m, at a road junction, the Sandstone Trail goes to the right. Keep straight ahead to descend past Rock House Farm and another road junction before reaching a crossroads at the bottom.

3. To visit the crafts centre, go straight ahead for 100m. Otherwise, turn right to head for the Pheasant Inn. Continue along Pennsylvania Lane, an attractive little cul-de-sac road along the bottom

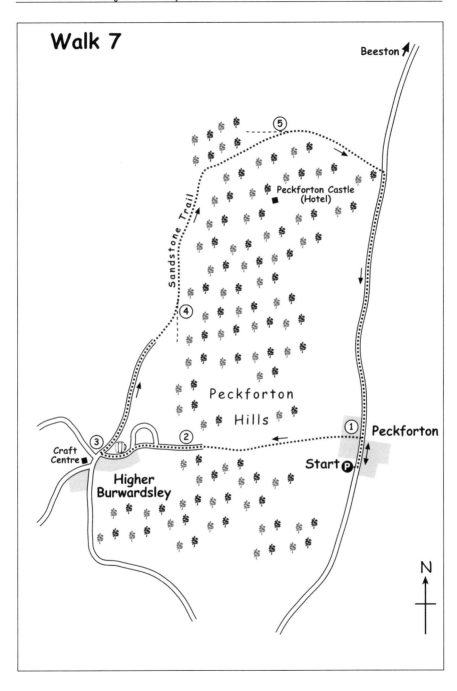

of the steep wooded scarp, passing a few scattered houses and ignoring any paths to right or left. At the end of the road is a locked gate, with (awkward) kissing gate beside. Continue along a good broad track rising fairly steeply through the woodland.

4. Join the Sandstone Way at a signpost, bearing left to follow 'Beeston Castle' along a good woodland track. Go straight ahead at a junction, through an open gate. At the far end of the woodland reach a locked gate with another awkward kissing gate beside. There is a 'Sandstone Trail' signpost.

5. Turn right, along a minor road, with woodland to the right and farming land to the left. There are splendid views of Beeston Castle. The Sandstone Trail turns off to the left towards Beeston Castle; continue along the minor road to reach a junction with a more important road, Stone House Lane. Turn right to walk by the roadside, passing the impressive entrance lodge to Peckforton Castle (hotel) on the right, before reaching the bottom of Hill Lane and then the right turn to the car park.

Walk 8: Grindley Brook and the Willeymoor Inn

Assessment: *Grade 1.*

A level out-and-back walk along the towpath of a section of the Llangollen branch of the Shropshire Union Canal.

Distance: 5km (3 miles).

Total ascent: A few metres at Grindley Brook locks.

Start/car parking: Across the canal from the Willeymoor Inn, there is a customers' car park. There is also space for cars along the side of the approach lane to this car park, grid reference 535451. Turn off the A49 to the west approximately 2 miles north of Whitchurch along a short lane signposted to Willeymoor,

Refreshments: Willeymoor Inn. Café at Grindley Brook locks. Horse and Jockey Inn at Grindley Brook.

Map: Ordnance Survey Explorer 257, Crewe and Nantwich, 1:25,000.

The Area

From its junction with the Shropshire Union main line at Hurleston, near Nantwich, to its terminus among the mountains of North Wales above Llangollen, the Llangollen branch is 46 miles long. It was originally part of an ambitious scheme by the celebrated Thomas Telford and William Jessop to link the rivers Severn, Dee and Mersey. There were various branches, including the Montgomeryshire Canal to Welshpool and Newtown, now closed. The Llangollen Canal has fortunately been kept open, mainly due to its importance as a water feed from the upper reaches of the River Dee to the junction at Hurleston, and has become one of the country's most popular canals for recreational boating. The aqueducts at Chirk and Pontcysyllte are among the finest surviving monuments to the canal age.

Grindley Brook has six locks, of which three form a staircase,

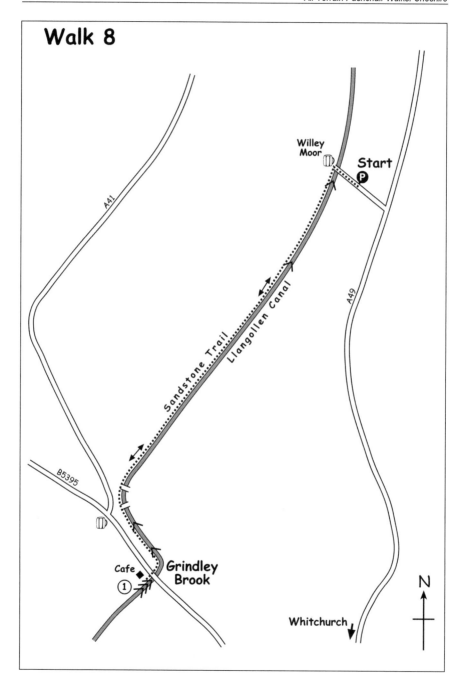

Walk 8

Willey Moor

Start
℗

A41

Sandstone Trail

Llangollen Canal

A49

B5395

Cafe
①

Grindley Brook

Whitchurch

N

adjacent to a right-angled turn under the A41 road. There is a lock outside the Willeymoor Inn.

The Walk

The Llangollen Canal, Grindley Brook

Cross the canal and turn left to follow the towpath. There is a 'Sandstone Trail' information board. This section of the towpath forms part of that long-distance route. Pass Povey's lock, then along a low embankment, with primroses in spring-time. Go under the nicely-proportioned bridge 26, which carries a footpath over the canal. After a mile-stone giving distances to Frodsham and to Whitchurch, go under a bridge (which carries the trackbed of a disused railway line) and approach the first Grindley Brook lock. There is an unusual book and craft shop close to this first lock. Go under another bridge and walk beside the locks and under the main road to the staircase of three locks, by the café and the 'Canal's Most Unusual Store'.

1. Return to Willeymoor by the same route.

Walk 9: Acton and the Shropshire Union Canal

Assessment: Grade 3.

A generally easy walk, but there are some steps to be negotiated and also one gate which requires ATPs to be lifted.

Distance: 6km (3¾ miles).

Total ascent: Negligible.

Start/car parking: Substantial free car park by the roadside in Acton, grid reference 632530.

Refreshments: Star Inn, Acton.

Map: Ordnance Survey Explorer 257, Crewe and Nantwich, 1:24,000.

The Area

Situated a short distance along the A534 to the north-west of Nantwich, Acton is a small, unremarkable, village. It does, however, have a good parish church, St Mary's, on the site of a Saxon church. The stone benches round the walls were provided for the elderly and infirm at a time when the more able-bodied members of the congregation had to stand, giving rise to the phrase 'the weakest go to the wall'.

Dorfold Hall, with its main entrance close to Acton village, is a Jacobean manor house built between 1615 and 1621 for Ralph Wilbraham, an influential Nantwich man. It is open to the public on one day each week and on Bank Holidays.

The main line of the Shropshire Union canal passes close to Nantwich before bending a little to the west to head for Chester and Ellesmere Port. There is a substantial marina approximately half a mile north-west of Nantwich, at the point where the original (wide) canal of 1774 terminated. Much later, in 1835, a (narrow) extension was constructed, to link up with the Birmingham canal system at

Nantwich Marina *(Photograph: Graham Beech)*

Autherley. Commercial traffic, including oil products and metals, continued into the 1960s. The canal, with its branch to Llangollen, is now very popular for recreational boating.

The Walk

Cross the A534 with care. Turn left to pass the Star Inn and two cottages before forking right along a wide track, leading to Dorfold Dairy Farm. Pass a gate and continue past a post with waymarks, including 'Crewe and Nantwich Circular Walk'. Go straight ahead at a crossing of tracks before traversing an area of open farming land. The large Dorfold Farm is passed; there is a waymark on a post. Reach locked double gates; there is a narrow gap beside the gates but ATPs will need to be lifted. Pass another gate before joining the public road, Dig Lane. Go straight ahead to join a more important road, Marsh Lane.

1. Turn left to walk by the roadside, passing two groups of dwellings on the right, then Marsh Lane House on the left.

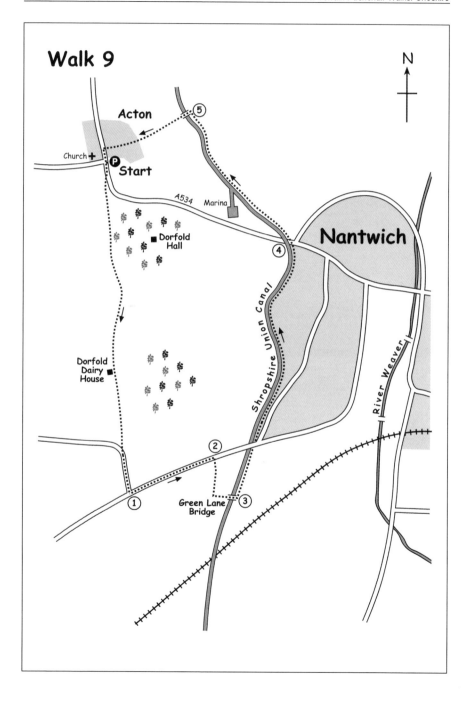

2. Turn right in a further 40m to follow a firm-surfaced farm track (no signpost), soon bending to the left to reach a bridge over the canal.

3. Descend eight steps to reach the towpath. Turn right to pass under the bridge and follow the towpath. Pass under bridge 91; the towpath now has a gravelled surface. Reach the first of a series of five small wooden sculptures which decorate this length of the canal. The canal is soon on an embankment, with a strong bend to the east, both necessitated by the need to avoid the grounds of Dorfold Hall. The then owner of the Hall was not cooperative when the canal was constructed. There are popular boat moorings along the canal side as the fringe of residential Nantwich is passed. The canal crosses the A534 on a high bridge; the lovely decorative metalwork can be seen only from the road below.

4. Continue round a left bend and past the extensive Nantwich Marina, which has boat hire and other canal-related activities including a café. Pass bridge 92, with a large wooden horse, (in 2007 a great deal of improvement work was in progress on the towpath and Acton Bridge).

5. At the next bridge, Acton Bridge, leave the canal up a few steps, cross back over the bridge and follow a path across a field, rising slightly towards residential development. Go up four steps to a gate and take a surfaced path between houses to a residential road, Wilbraham Road. Bear right to reach the main A534 in a short distance. Turn left by the roadside to return to the car park.

Walk 10: Nantwich

Assessment: Grade 1 or Grade 3.

There are two versions of this pleasant walk; both start and finish close to the Nantwich town centre. Both use the Shropshire Union Canal on the outward route but the longer walk (a) traverses a rural area to the south of the town, with a fair distance over roughish grass, before heading back through the parkland adjacent to the River Weaver. The shorter route (b) avoids this rural area, using a residential road as a short cut to the parkland.

Distance: (a) 5.3km (3¼ miles) (b) 3.5km (2¼ miles).

Total ascent: Negligible.

Start/car parking: There are several pay and display car parks close to the bridge which carries the A534 across the River Weaver. Best, but not easy to find, is a free car park behind the properties on the south side, about 150–200m to the west of the river bridge, grid reference 649524.

Refreshments: Choice in town centre.

Map: Ordnance Survey Explorer 257, Crewe and Nantwich, 1:25,000.

The Area

Nantwich is a fine little town, rich in traditional 'black-and-white' Cheshire buildings, including Churche's Mansion of 1577. The array of individual shops is enhanced by pedestrianisation of much of the centre. The great parish church of St Mary – the 'Cathedral of South Cheshire' – with central octagonal tower, is rightly esteemed. There is much fine carving in the choir stalls and elsewhere in the church. The town's early wealth was founded on the salt trade but this had faded away by the mid-19th century. The town was devastated by a great fire in 1583/4, which burned for twenty days. One of the decisive battles of the civil war was fought at Nantwich in 1644, the Parliamentarian victory crushing any Royalist hopes of a change of fortune.

The Shropshire Union Canal is described in walk no.9.

Dorfold Hall, beside the A532, close to Acton, is a Jacobean manor house of 1615-21 for Ralph Wilbraham, an influential Nantwich man. During the summer season it is open to the public on one day each week, plus Bank Holidays.

Welsh Row, Nantwich

The Walk

From the road bridge over the River Weaver, start along Welsh Row, the A534, heading out of town. There are lovely black-and-white and other fine buildings along this road. The Widows' Almshouses, the site of a house where King James I lodged and Malthouse Cottages are of particular interest.

1. At a major road junction in half a mile, go across towards the canal on its high embankment; the bridge carrying the canal over A534 is particularly fine. Bear right to ascend a long, gentle, ramp leading to the canal towpath. Turn sharp left at the top of the ramp to walk along the towpath, over the bridge. The canal passes close to the residential fringe of Nantwich, with extensive boat moorings, bending to avoid the grounds of Dorfold Hall, which is out of sight.

2. For (b) the shorter walk, leave the towpath about 150m before a bridge, bearing left on a surfaced path down the bank to a resi-

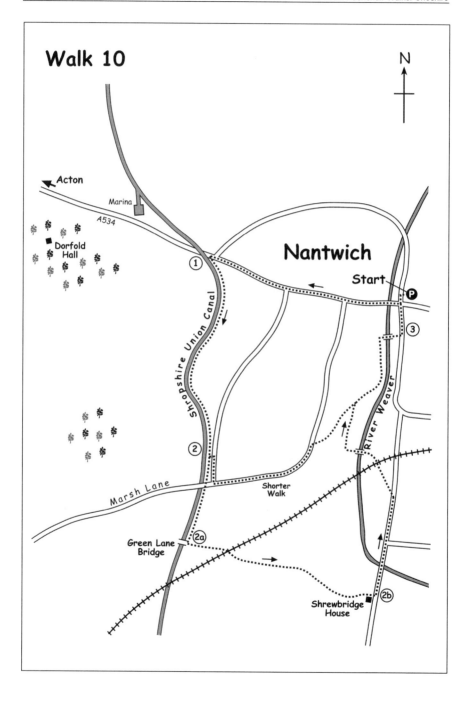

Walk 10

N

Acton

Marina

A534

Dorfold
Hall

Shropshire Union Canal

Nantwich

Start

P

③

River Weaver

①

②

Marsh Lane

Shorter
Walk

Green Lane
Bridge

②a

②b

Shrewbridge
House

dential road. Bear right for 100m or so to a road junction. Turn left to follow this road for a little less than half a mile. As the road bends to the left to skirt the parkland by the River Weaver, bear right along one of the surfaced tracks which head generally north, parallel with the river. Keep the river close on the right before crossing Mill Bridge, about 150m south of the road bridge.

3. Turn left to walk to the road bridge and cross that bridge to return to the car park.

For the longer walk – (a) 5.3km (3¼ miles) – continue along the towpath past point 2, going under a bridge in approximately 150m and then:

2a. Leave the canal at the next bridge, Green Lane Bridge, go up a few steps and through a little gate ahead. Follow the field edge path, descending gently. Go through another gate, pass a little pond on the right, and cross the railway line, with gates on either side. Go through another gate, then through a gate into an area of cattle pens. To left and right is the line of the former Crewe to Market Drayton railway line, closed in 1967. Continue ahead, along the edge of another field, before bearing right to pass a waymarked post in the middle of the field. Descend to cross a little stream on a gated bridge. Cross the next field, passing another waymarked post in the middle. Go through a gate to reach the road, A530.

2b. Turn left to walk by the roadside; as the A530 turns to the right, go straight ahead. In about 200m, before a terrace of houses, turn left along a surfaced track descending gently to pass under the railway line. Cross the River Weaver on a long footbridge and bear right to head through the riverside parkland. Bear right at a junction of paths to stay beside the river, soon reaching Mill Bridge. Cross to rejoin the shorter route at point 3.

Walk 11: Little Budworth Country Park

Assessment: *Grade 2.*

This almost level walk has one rise and some soft sand underfoot.

Distance: 3km (2 miles).

Total ascent: Less than 10m (33ft).

Start/car parking: As for the Little Budworth walk – no.12.

Refreshments: None en route but the two inns at Little Budworth are not far away.

Map: Ordnance Survey Explorer 267, Northwich and Delamere Forest, 1:25,000.

The Area

Little Budworth Country Park is part of a formerly larger area of heathland, now much reduced by progressive enclosure and conversion to agriculture. Despite being well wooded, the Country Park has surviving areas of heather and also hollows with wet heath, mire and pond. These heathland areas are being maintained and occasionally extended. The wildlife is rich and distinctive, including squirrels, grass snakes, lizards, pipits, warblers and all three species of woodpecker. There is unlimited public access to the Country Park, on well-used trails throughout.

The Walk

This circuit is largely marked by red arrows on posts. Pass the barrier to follow an inviting woodland track close to the right-hand edge of the woodland, with a field a short distance to the right, where there is also a large house. Silver birch are the predominant trees. Pass a gate. The track narrows slightly as gorse becomes the dominant shrub.

Little Budworth Country Park

1. Cross a tarmac house access road (red arrow) and continue.
   Cross another roadway (red arrow) before reaching a 'T' junction (A left turn here provides a shorter circuit). Turn right to
   continue (red arrow). At a junction of several paths go straight
   ahead (red arrow), descending a little to an attractive pond on
   the left. After the pond, the red arrow points to the left, where
   there are steps. Ignore this; go straight ahead, uphill, to a stile
   with a 'duck under' barrier. Pass close to a house on the right and
   continue along a lane to reach Beech Road in 150m.

2. Turn left to walk by the roadside; there is a large house to the
   right. Cross Coach Road to an earth roadway opposite, with a
   'restricted byway' sign.

3. Immediately before the far end of the woodland on the left, turn
   left at a 'public footpath' sign to follow a good path winding
   through the trees. There is a field 20m to the right. There is a red
   arrow as a track joins from the left. Cross over a major roadway.
   Any further junctions have a red arrow, generally pointing

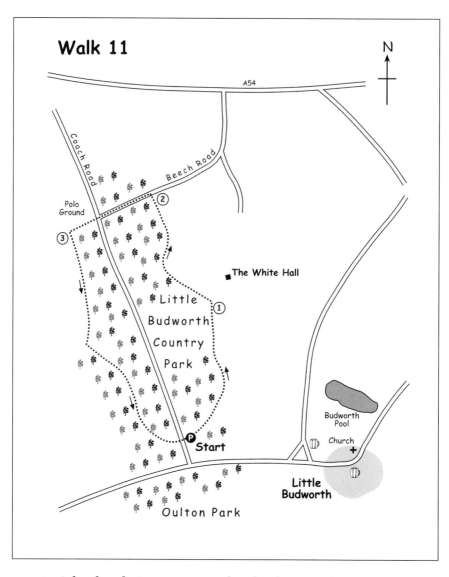

straight ahead. At a crossing of paths there is a log with a carved dragon's head; go ahead at the adjacent junction, with a road now quite close on the right. Cross Coach Road to return to the car park.

Walk 12: Little Budworth

Assessment: *Grade 3.*

Not a difficult walk, but the grading reflects a combination of length, some uphill and sandy surfaces.

Distance: 6.5km (4 miles).

Total ascent: Less than 40m (131ft).

Start/car parking: Free car park with public conveniences, Little Budworth Country Park, about half a mile west of Little Budworth village. From the village, pass two road junctions before turning right at Coach Road, almost opposite a gateway into Oulton Park. The car park is on the right in about 200m, grid reference 590655.

Refreshments: Red Lion Inn, Little Budworth.

Map: Ordnance Survey Explorer 267, Northwich and Delamere Forest, 1:25,000.

The Area

Whilst not rivalling its 'Great' counterpart as a showpiece village, Little Budworth is a pleasant place, with church and inn facing one another across the main street. Most of this excellent circuit is around the perimeter of Little Budworth Country Park, also passing close to the very different Oulton Park, a long-established motor-racing track, best avoided on racing days.

The country park is a surviving portion of a formerly much larger area of heathland (ref. walk no.11) and is now largely wooded.

The Walk

From the car park cross the road, turning left at once along a sandy track through the trees, parallel with the Coach Road. Reach the public road almost opposite the impressive Oulton Park entrance.

1.   Cross the road and turn right to join a path through the trees, not

immediately apparent. The Oulton Park boundary fence is soon close on the left. Cross an Oulton Park access road and continue along the path on the far side. The path angles to join the public road. Cross over.

2. Follow a broad, unsurfaced roadway with a 'restricted byway' sign. In 40m bear left at a fork. The roadway keeps to the edge of the woodland of the Country Park, rising very gently, with farm-land to the left. In spring there are clumps of bluebells along the way, with plenty of activity by rabbits.

3. At a crossing of paths, with more 'restricted byway' signs, turn right along a track between high hedges; the sandy ground here might make pushing a little harder. Reach woodland and approach a public road. Go straight across to walk along the side of a tarmac road.

4. In less than 300m turn right along a broad track; there is a 'Whitehall Lane and Coach Road' sign round the corner. Pass close to a house on the left and descend to a stile, with a 'duck under' barrier beside. Pass an attractive little pool on the right, soon reaching a fork. Keep left, then left again in a further 5m along a woodland path, with a field boundary fence about 30m to the left. Join a wide track and continue, downhill, bearing left in front of a house. Pass a pond on the left, reaching a junction of paths. Go ahead, bearing right, gently uphill along a sunken lane, soon reaching tarmac. Pass a pair of semi-detached houses.

5. In a short distance turn right along a tarmac track. As the track turns sharp right, go left along an earth track between hedges to a 'T' junction. Turn right along a similar track to reach the public road.

6. Turn right, then left in 20m to follow a broad track. At a junction with field entrances, go ahead; the path is now narrow, but adequate. Soon, there are glimpses of Little Budworth church (see next page) over Budworth Pool.

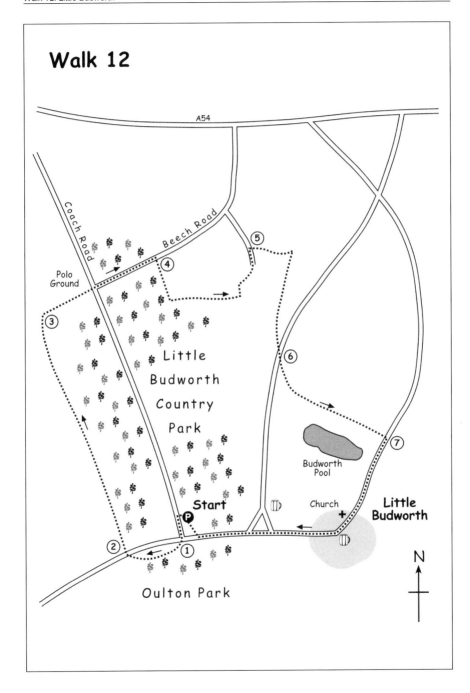

7. At the next public road turn right to walk by the roadside towards the village. Pass the foot of Budworth Pool and an apparent former mill site on the left before passing the Post Office/stores. Stay with the main road at a junction and continue, with the church on the right and the inn on the left. Pass the village hall, then two road junctions. After the second junction, there is a path through the wood-

Little Budworth church

land on the right which leads directly back to the car park. Alternatively, continue to the junction with the Coach Road and turn right.

Walk 13: Whitegate Way

Assessment: Grade 1.

A short, virtually level, walk on good surfaces. No difficulties, but a choice between squeezing through a narrow gap or lifting over a low barrier.

Distance: 4km (2½ miles).

Total ascent: Negligible.

Start/car parking: Free car park at the former Whitegate station, grid reference 615680. Signposted from the A54 and situated a little more than one mile north of that road. Leave the A54 two miles east of its junction with the A49.

Refreshments: None, but a potential picnic site by the side of a lake.

Map: Ordnance Survey Explorer 267, Northwich and Delamere Forest, 1:25,000.

The Area

The Whitegate Way uses the trackbed of the former Cheshire Lines branch railway line which connected Winsford with the main Manchester to Chester line at Cuddington. The construction of the six-mile line was motivated by the lucrative salt trade at Winsford. It was single track throughout, with a passing loop at Whitegate, the only intermediate station. From its opening on the 1st June 1870 it was never as successful as anticipated. Winsford was already served by the powerful L.N.W.R. on its east side. The passenger service, discontinued no less than three times throughout the line's history, was at best perfunctory. Final closure was in 1966. The line now provides a fine route for walkers, cyclist and horse riders, a managed wildlife corridor, with spring and summer flowers, birds and butterflies.

The adjacent lakes were, like so many in central Cheshire, formed by land subsidence following the underground extraction of salt as brine.

The Whitegate Way

The Walk

At the information board by the former station, turn left, along the trackbed. Pass below the edge of the old platform and continue under the extensively propped road bridge. There is a signpost 'Cuddington 4.7km Delamere Forest 9km'. The track surface is excellent as it rises very gently. Pass a caravan site and a seat before reaching Newchurch Crossing, one of only two places on the Way where sections of rail can still be seen. There is another Cuddington and Delamere Forest signpost.

1. Here, there is a choice. Either go ahead for a further 100m before turning right; an upright post then poses a possible problem for ATPs or turn right at the crossing then immediately left, lifting the ATP over a low (2ft) barrier before following a grass path to rejoin the circuit. The route continues past a possible lakeside picnic spot, along a good grass path to a stile with 'duck under' barrier. After the barrier there is another stile ahead. Avoid this by bearing right to another 'duck under' barrier at an anglers' locked gate.

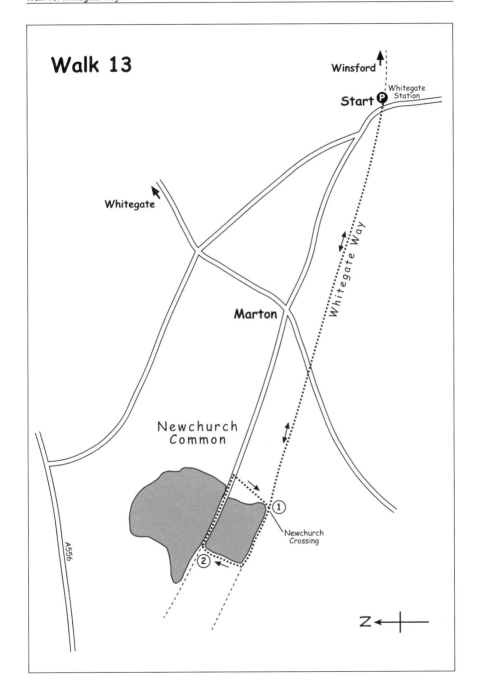

Walk 13

Winsford

Whitegate
Station

Start Ⓟ

Whitegate

Marton

Whitegate Way

Newchurch
Common

① Newchurch
Crossing

②

A556

N

2.   Turn right to follow an unsurfaced roadway between two lakes; just glimpsed through the trees; the Warrington Anglers' Association has the fishing rights. Ignore footpaths right and left. In a further 60m at a widened area, take a wide track raking back to the right. There is no signpost; across the field to the left are bungalows. The track soon bends to the left, with extensive rabbit burrows alongside. At Newchurch Crossing, point 1, turn left to return along the Way to the car park.

Walk 14: Weaver Parkway and Newbridge

Assessment: Grade 2.

Generally easy walking with good surfaces, including some tarmac. A little rise and fall and three gateways which could be a little awkward, but are likely to be changed in the near future. A section of the track is close to deep water, potentially dangerous for young children.

Distance: 4.5km (2¾ miles).

Total ascent: 15m (49ft).

Start/car parking: Small free car park accessed directly from A5018, Winsford to Northwich road – a left turn almost opposite Morrison's supermarket, grid reference 656669. Note possible early closing time!

Refreshments: None. Picnic area at Newbridge.

Map: Ordnance Survey Explorer 267, Northwich and Delamere Forest, 1:25,000.

The Area

For much of this walk the surroundings are not entirely pretty, with a working mine which supplies rock salt for the whole of Britain dominating one side of the waterway. However, much of this former industrial landscape has been imaginatively reclaimed, particularly at the Winsford End, where the Weaver Parkway includes a trail for the disabled and National Cycle Route 5 forms the basis of the present walk.

In this part of the Weaver Valley, centuries of salt extraction have resulted in an environment which encourages the growth of salt-tolerant plants such as sea milkwort, sea aster and scentless mayweed. The land subsidence consequent on extracting brine has resulted in numerous scattered ponds, with a rich diversity of pond life. The area is now managed to enhance its wildlife value.

The Weaver Parkway

Much of the River Weaver was canalised in the 19th century as the 'Weaver Navigation' in order to permit sizeable craft to serve the major salt and chemical industries of Northwich and the salt industry of Winsford. The northern end of the waterway connects with the Manchester Ship Canal and the River Mersey. The picnic area at Newbridge has both fixed and swing bridges across the Navigation, the latter opening to allow the passage of large vessels.

The Walk

Leave the car park through a kissing gate. Fork right in 20m along a narrow path, bearing right. Go through a gateway, cross the access road to the AMCOL factory and through a similar gate on the far side. In 30m do not join the more major track on the left but bear right, rising gently, to pass an interesting modern sculpture of bicycles.

1.   Join the main track, wide with a good surface. At a fork go either left or right. A track joins on the left and the river comes into view, as do huge heaps of salt on the far side. Pass through a

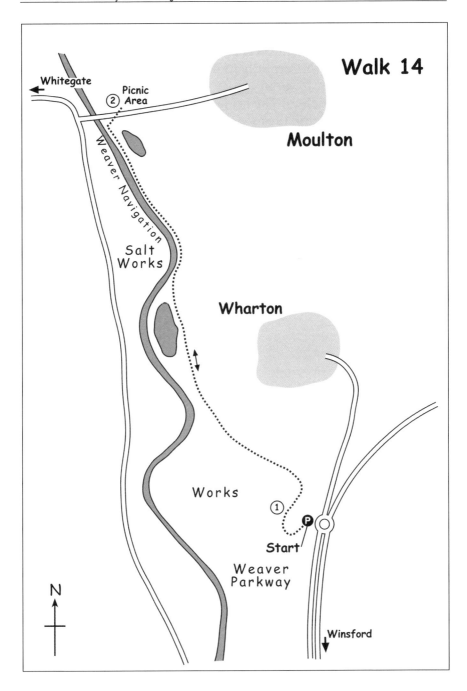

Walk 14

Whitegate

Picnic
② Area

Moulton

Weaver Navigation

Salt
Works

Wharton

Works

①

Start

Weaver
Parkway

N

Winsford

wooded area, with a most unusual metal seat. Stay with the main track at a crossing. There is a large pond below to the left. Across the river the formerly important wharves serving the salt mine now seem to be in a poor state of repair. Keep straight ahead at any junction. The bridges close to the picnic area come into view ahead and the area, with car parking and road access to Moulton village and to a minor road to the west, is soon reached.

2. Return by the same route. There is scope for some variation, particularly a section where a path goes between the large pond and the river.

Walk 15: Moulton and Vale Royal Locks

Assessment: *Grade 3.*

A fair amount of ascent, a stile and an awkward kissing gate. The return path is along the side of deep water, not recommended for young children.

Distance: 5km (3 miles).

Total ascent: 30m (98ft)

Start/car parking: Newbridge informal picnic area by the side of a swing bridge across the Weaver Navigation. Accessed either from the Whitegate to Winsford road (from west) or from Moulton down an unsurfaced road from the southern corner of the village, grid reference 652688.

Refreshments: None.

Map: Ordnance Survey Explorer 267, Northwich and Delamere Forest, 1:25,000.

The Area

This circular walk links the village of Moulton with the Weaver Navigation and its locks. Moulton is a sprawling village, sitting above the bank of the Weaver, separated from the Navigation by the West Coast main railway line. There is an old main street, surrounded by large modern residential areas. The Weaver Navigation has a deep wide channel (Vale Royal Cut), dug to allow large commercial vessels from the River Mersey to reach the industrial areas of Northwich and Winsford. The side-by-side locks have swing bridges.

At Newbridge picnic area there is one swing and one fixed bridge across the water. To the west of the Weaver Valley is the site of the former Vale Royal Abbey.

The Weaver Navigation

The Walk

Start by walking up the unsurfaced roadway signposted 'public foot-path. cycleway 5', riding steadily under a substantial railway bridge, probably formerly carrying a branch line into a works area. The site is now a static caravan park. Pass under another railway bridge – the West Coast main line – and continue rising, now through farming land, with Moulton village in view.

1. On reaching the built-up area, turn left at a 'restricted byway' sign to follow an unsurfaced roadway along the edge of the village. As the roadway turns left to Bank Farm, continue ahead along a narrower track. There are long views to the far side of the Weaver Valley. Reach the far end of the village. To the right is the main street. Go ahead through a gate with a 'footpath Northwich' sign. Pass close to a large farm on the right before reaching a junction.

2. Turn left to follow a 'public footpath River Weaver' sign, along a broad lane. Cross a bridge over the railway line and reach the end of the lane at a farm gate. Continue along an earth/grass path, soon on a reserved strip between cultivated fields, gener-

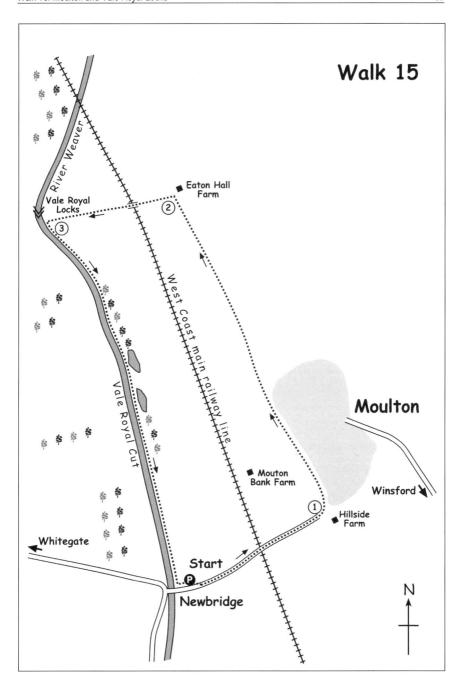

Walk 15

River Weaver

Eaton Hall Farm

Vale Royal Locks

②

③

West Coast main railway line

Vale Royal Cut

Moulton

Winsford

Mouton Bank Farm

①

Hillside Farm

Whitegate

Start

P

Newbridge

N

ally downhill into the Weaver Valley. Go through a gate/awkward kissing gate at the bottom to join the waterside path.

3. Turn left but, for a closer look at the mighty locks, detour to the right for 50m to a lock-keeper's building and an information board. Head back towards Newbridge along the river path, generally good but often very close to deep water. There are three stiles, which can be avoided by ducking under a bar at the side. A series of ponds to the left provides a rich wild life habitat. Pass a seat and 'Vale Royal Visitor Moorings'. A short distance before regaining the Newbridge picnic area is another stile, at which lifting an ATP cannot be avoided. Continue to the parking area.

Walk 16: Marbury Country Park

Assessment: Grade 3.

The walk is longer than most in the book, there is a small amount of ascent and there are steps, including a footbridge over the canal.

Distance: 5.5km (3½ miles).

Total ascent: 20m (66ft).

Start/car parking: Large pay and display car park for the Anderton Lift and the Anderton Visitor Park. Well signposted from the Barnton to Comberbatch minor road. Approximately two miles from the centre of Northwich, via A533, grid reference 650754.

Refreshments: Café at visitor centre.

Map: Ordnance Survey Explorer 267, Northwich and Delamere Forest, 1:25,000.

The Area

Until comparatively recent times, Northwich was a great centre of the Cheshire salt industry, which consisted largely of the pumping of brine from below ground. Imperial Chemical Industries (ICI) has large industrial premises in Northwich, facing the visitor centre across the River Weaver. Much of the former industrial dereliction has now been attractively transformed. Northwich Community Woodland includes Marbury Country Park, the Anderton Nature Park and other reclaimed land, all well-managed as a comprehensive recreational area. As would be expected in an area formerly subjected to brine extraction, there are numerous ponds and small lakes.

Budworth Mere forms the northern boundary, whilst the Trent and Mersey Canal, with a large marina and plenty of boating activity, threads its way through the Park

A swimming pool, children's play area and arboretum are included in the Park.

The Anderton Boat Lift

The well-varied flora and fauna, which include some species which are particularly tolerant of salt, are described in a leaflet obtainable from the visitor centre. There are bird-watching hides close to Budworth Mere.

The Walk

Head down towards the boat lift and the visitor centre building. At the bottom of the slope turn sharp right to follow the well-surfaced towpath of the canal, passing moored boats and under a bridge before reaching Anderton Marina, on both sides of the canal. Go under a road bridge and then rise to cross a bridge over a waterway linking separate parts of the marina. Continue along an embankment and under a road bridge (Marbury Lane) before approaching a footbridge. Go through a squeezer, under the bridge and then turn back right for a few metres to ascend the not too difficult steps and cross the bridge.

1. Bear right on the far side of the canal. In 100m bear left, away from the canal. There is a sign 'Mere. Information Office'. Ignore a track on the left; continue through Big Wood on a fine wood-

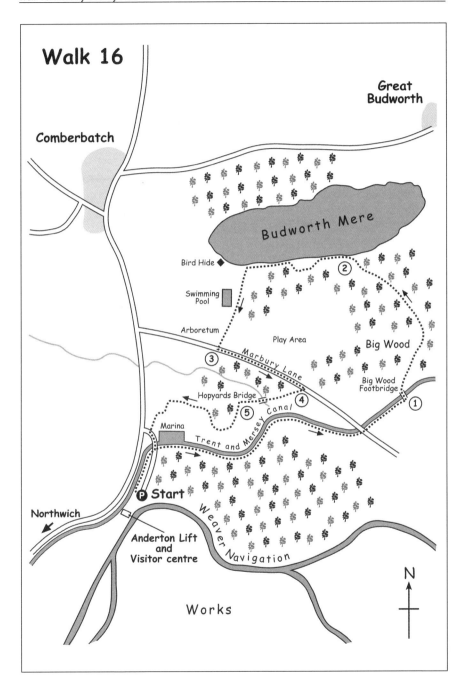

Walk 16

Comberbatch

Great
Budworth

Budworth Mere

Bird Hide ◆

Swimming
Pool

Arboretum

Play Area

Big Wood

②

③

Marbury Lane

Big Wood
Footbridge

Hopyards Bridge

④

①

⑤

Canal

Marina

Trent and Mersey

Ⓟ Start

Northwich

Anderton Lift
and
Visitor centre

Weaver Navigation

Works

N

land path. In springtime there are magnificent bluebells. Ignore a track on the right. There is soon a stream below to the right, then a wonderfully carved wooden seat – how many animals can you identify? At a 'T' junction follow 'Mere. Car Park' to the right. Budworth Mare is soon visible through the trees. At a fork, the main track goes uphill. Take the lesser track, to the right. In 40m, by a little pool, turn left, soon passing a little footbridge on the right. Do not cross.

2. Carry on, now along the shore of Budworth Mere, a most attractive lake, with Great Budworth church in view. Stay with the track as it turn left, away from the shore, for 30m to a 'T' junction. Turn right, gently uphill. In 100m fork right by a seat to go downhill back to the shore. Continue until 50m short of a boathouse then go left, uphill. Go left again in 40m still rising, to reach a tarmac roadway. Go straight ahead at a 'car park' signpost. Pass a large open area with avenues of lime trees. There may be craft stalls and other attractions. Pass public conveniences, bearing left to a signpost. Follow 'swimming pool and arboretum' along a tarmac roadway. The car park and children's play area are to the left, the swimming pool and arboretum to the right.

3. Turn left along a public road (Marbury Lane) 'No entry for vehicles'. Follow the road for 500m.

4. Turn right at the point where a track crosses the road (to the left are gates), taking the right-hand of two tracks, soon descending through woodland, then down a few steps. Reach the stream at the bottom of the valley, bearing right to cross a little bridge (Hopyards Bridge). Ascend zig zags up the far side of the valley to reach a 'T' junction by a seat.

5. Turn left to take a good but winding track; there are ponds and the canal to the left. Pass an area of recent tree planting (Hopyards Wood). Approach the public road, go left at a fork, then past a barrier to cross the Marina car park. Reach the access road to the visitor centre car park; turn left, cross the bridge over the canal then turn right towards 'Anderton Nature Park and Boat Lift'. Descend to the canal tow path to return to the car park.

Walk 17: Great Budworth

Assessment: Grade2.

A simple little, almost level, circuit. Grade 2 only because of possibly rather long grass on the field part of the route.

Distance: 2.8km (1¾ miles)

Total ascent: 15m (49ft).

Start/car parking: Roadside verge near the junction of Belmont Road and a road signposted to Warrington and Antrobus, due north of Great Budworth village, grid reference 660783.

Refreshments: Ice Cream Farm, with tea shop and light snacks. George and Dragon Inn, Great Budworth.

Map: Ordnance Survey Explorer 267, Northwich and Delamere Forest, 1:25,000.

The Area

Great Budworth ranks very highly among the most charming villages in Cheshire, liberally endowed with timber-framed black-and-white cottages clustering around the sandstone church and the inn. The village was obviously built well before the motor age and a visit on foot is highly recommended.

New Westage Farm is rather unusual in having home-made ice cream as its principal product. The tea shop, with inside and outside seating, is very family orientated.

The Walk

Start along a wide farm access roadway to a waymarked (open) gate/stile. The track is level and Gt. Budworth church is in view ahead. Go through an open gate and cross a field, possibly a little muddy. After a waymarked stile/gate continue along a path at the edge of a field. Cross a narrow field to a waymarked gate/stile. Follow the direction of the arrow, turning left here. The fence/hedge is now on the left, as the path descends gently to another waymarked gate/stile. There are two more gate/stiles and another meadow to cross before joining a little lane.

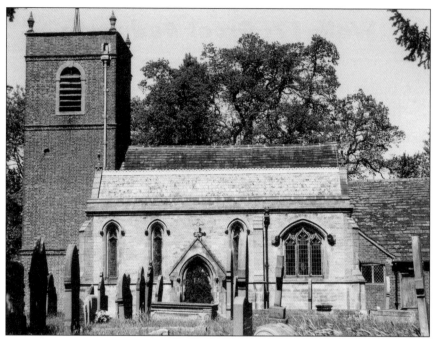

Great Budworth church

1. Turn left, gently uphill, to walk into the village, heading directly
    for the church. Pass the Parish Hall on the left and the bowling
    green on the right before reaching the centre. After any explora-
    tion and/or refreshment at the inn, turn left immediately in front
    of the church into School lane, a most attractive cobbled street.
    There is a 'public footpath' sign. Pass the school and go through
    a gate. There is a 'duck under' bar for ATPs. Continue along a
    tree-lined avenue, with daffodils, ransomes and other spring
    flowers. Go through another waymarked gate and turn left along
    an unsurfaced roadway to walk to the public road.

2. Cross over to a signpost 'Antrobus and Warrington' and an Ice
    Cream Farm notice. Walk along the roadside, reaching the ice
    cream farm in about 200m. After the farm, carry on along the
    road (Heath Lane) to its junction with Belmont Road.

3. Turn left to walk along the roadside back to the parking place.

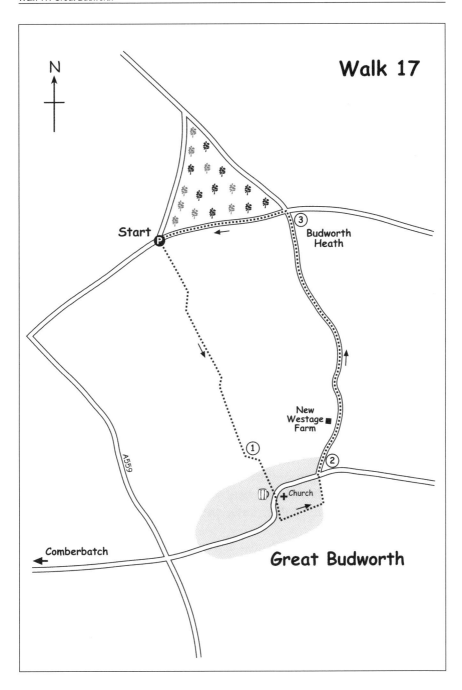

N

Walk 17

Start

Budworth
Heath

③

①

New
Westage ■
Farm

②

A559

Church

Comberbatch

Great Budworth

Walk 18: Delamere Forest

Assessment: *Grade 3.*

There are no particular difficulties, but a fair amount of rise and fall and some soft, sandy, surfaces.

Distance: 4.5km (2¾ miles).

Total ascent: 30m (98ft).

Start/car parking: Pay and display car park at the main Delamere Forest visitor centre, close to the railway station, approached from the B5152, grid reference 552704.

Refreshments: Café at the visitor centre.

Map: Ordnance Survey Explorer 267, Northwich and Delamere Forest, 1:25,000.

The Area

Delamere Forest is a 2400-acre surviving remnant of the former great forest of Mara and Mondrum, hunting ground for the Earls of Chester, becoming a royal possession of King Edward III in the 14th century. Long in the ownership of the Forestry Commission, there is now extensive public access to this rolling, largely wooded area, criss-crossed by forest roadways and trails. Blakemere Moss is a large reedy lake, frequented by large numbers of water fowl.

The comprehensive visitor centre has all the expected facilities, such as information centre, café, picnic area and public conveniences.

'Go Ape' is a 'high wire forest adventure' – a complex linkage of ladders and walkways high above the ground, recently added to the forest attractions. There are strict rules, such as a minimum age of 10 years and height and weight limitations.

The Walk

Walk back along the visitor centre access road, rising before turning

A track through the forest

left to cross the bridge over the railway. There is a large post labelled 'forest trails'. The various recommended routes are colour coded – the red trail coincides with most, but not all of our circuit.

1. Turn right in 20m to descend along an earth track, passing the 'Go Ape' booking hut and entering coniferous woodland. Various parts of the 'Go Ape' walkways are apparent in the trees. There is a red marker and a 'Delamere Way' waymark. As the track rises towards the public road, fork left (red marker) along a narrower track, delightfully close to the shore of Blakemere Moss, with its abundant bird life. The road is close on the right.

2. At a major junction after the lake, go straight ahead (red marker), steadily uphill. Turn left at a 'T' junction at the top (red marker), soon descending gently towards the lake. At a fork 50m short of the lake, go right (red marker) up a short, fairly steep rise. Go left at a fork (red marker), downhill. Join a more major track, beside a seat in less than 100m.

3. Turn right to reach a major junction, with picnic table, seats and

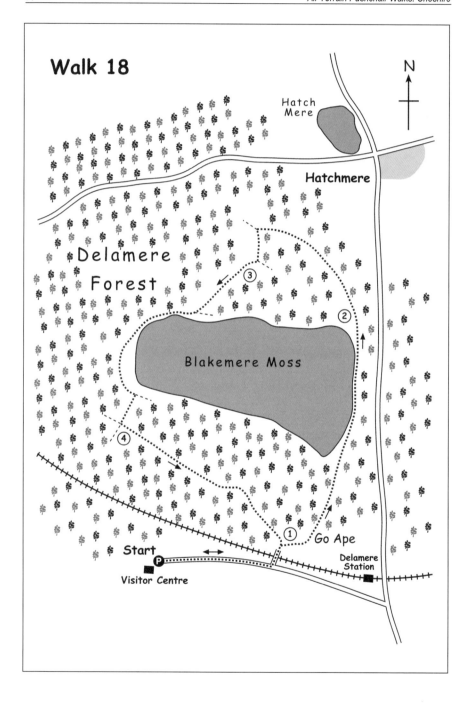

Walk 18

N

Hatch Mere

Hatchmere

Delamere Forest

③

②

Blakemere Moss

④

Go Ape

①

Start

Delamere Station

Visitor Centre

signposts. Go straight ahead to follow 'Linmere, cycle track, Delamere Way'. We are now leaving the 'red marker' route, following blue and white markers and a 'Delamere Way' waymark. Continue to a major junction; turn right (white and blue marker) to reach another major junction in 200m with a 'visitor centre' sign.

4. Turn left to follow the broad roadway, descending and bearing right (blue and white marker) at the next junction. The way back is now straightforward; the visitor centre buildings come into view before rejoining the outward route just short of the railway bridge. Cross the bridge and turn right to return to the car park.

Walk 19: Tatton Park

Assessment: Grade 1.

An almost level walk, on good surfaces throughout, with no stiles or other impediments

Distance: 5.3km (3¼ miles).

Total ascent: 18m (59ft).

Start/car parking: Main car park by the 'Mansion' (Tatton Hall) at Tatton Park, grid reference 744817. Park entrances at the north end and at the Knutsford end, well-signposted. Note – even National Trust members must pay an entrance charge for a vehicle.

Refreshments: Café in hall outbuildings.

Map: Ordnance Survey Explorer 268, Wilmslow, Macclesfield and Congleton, 1:25,000.

The Area

Tatton Park is an impressive historic estate including a deer park, of about 1000 acres in total, now managed by the National Trust. The multiple attractions include a stately home, gardens, specialist shop, café, recommended walking routes in the park and an adventure playground.

During the summer season there is a programme of events.

The Walk

From the main car park head towards the information board (there is a kiosk to the right). Bear left to and through the stable yard, where many of the facilities are found. Continue towards the 'mansion', left of the 'housekeeper's store' and under an arch into the courtyard. Bear left to exit through a gate and reach the access roadway. Turn right; there is a pond to the left.

1. Just before the road forks, turn right to follow an earth track

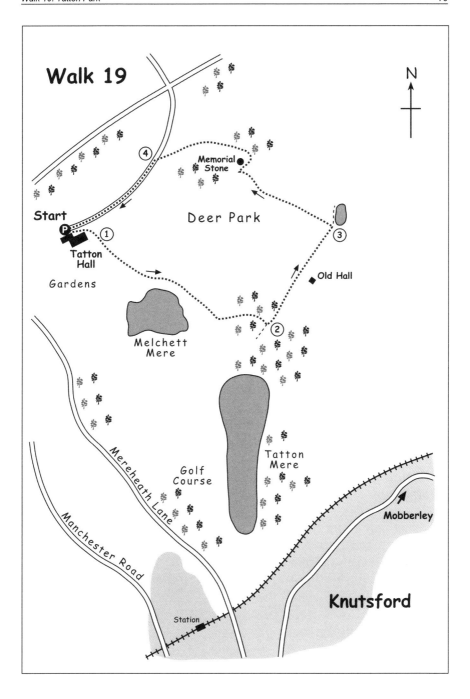

among trees, angling away from the boundary of the garden to the right. Approach Melchett Mere, keeping well to the left of this attractive lake. Pass a seat and cross the Knutsford access road diagonally to a seat. Ignore a track to the left and head for trees. Follow a narrow path through this belt of woodland.

2. Join a surfaced roadway, turning left, gently uphill. Pass Old Hall car park, the roadway now gravel surfaced. Pass a track to the right leading to the Old Hall and continue until Mill Pool is in sight, ahead.

3. One hundred metres short of the pool turn left along a grass track heading for an area of recent planting. Keep left at a fork and go across other tracks. Pass a gate and notice (the recent planting, to the right, is the deer-fenced Millennium Wood), rising gently. Pass a tiny pond and cross another track. The Airborne Forces monument is now in view; bear right to reach the monument, well-provided with seats. Continue along the gravel roadway to the right, soon bending to the left to join the main access drive. This area is a favourite of the herds of fallow deer which roam in the park.

4. Turn left along the access drive to return to the main Tatton Hall complex and the car park; there is a marked track through the trees to the left of the tarmac roadway.

Tatton Park: the Stable Yard

Walk 20: Styal Country Park

Assessment: *Grade 2 (to village). Grade 1 (to mill).*

No particular problems, good surfaces, but a long uphill push after passing the mill.

Distance: 4km (2½ miles), Grade 2 or 2.8km (1¾ miles), Grade 1.

Total ascent: 25m (82ft).

Start/car parking: Free car park with public conveniences by the side of B5166, Wilmslow to Wythenshawe road, grid reference 840822 or, free for National Trust members, the large official car park for Quarry Bank Mill, entered a short distance further north along B5166.

Refreshments: Café at Quarry Bank Mill.

Map: Ordnance Survey Explorer 268, Wilmslow, Macclesfield and Congleton, 1:25,000.

The Area

The Styal Country Park, which includes Quarry Bank Mill, the Apprentice House and Styal village, is owned and managed by the National Trust. It is a large scale visitor attraction to which members of the Trust have free access. For non-members, entry by car, to the mill and to the Apprentice House is charged.

For those with an interest in industrial archaeology, the mill is magnificent. Started in 1784 in what had been a completely rural part of the valley of the River Bollin, it was owned by generations of the Greg family, cotton manufacturers for 175 years. The largest working water wheel in Europe is still coupled to operational machinery.

Of intriguing sociological interest, the Apprentice House was home to up to 90 young people, mainly pauper children of 9 years of age upwards, at a time. Perhaps surprisingly, most of the apprentices were girls. The comparatively enlightened regime ensured that the children were fed and clothed, given basic education and an

Styal village

eventual job in the mill. The nearby village was constructed to house the workers.

The valley of the River Bollin, despite its proximity to Manchester suburbs, has attractive walks, including the section included in the present route.

The Walk

From the roadside car park, head along the track to the side of the public conveniences to a bridge over the River Dane.

1. Cross the bridge and turn left through a kissing gate to follow a path, generally by the side of the River Bollin. At a junction bear right, passing an embedded 'glacial erratic' stone. There are wild flowers in profusion including bluebells. Pass an area of wetland ('carr woodland'), on the left, where plants and then trees are reclaiming the land from the water. Cross Heron's Pool Bridge, pass a former quarry; parts of the mill were built using

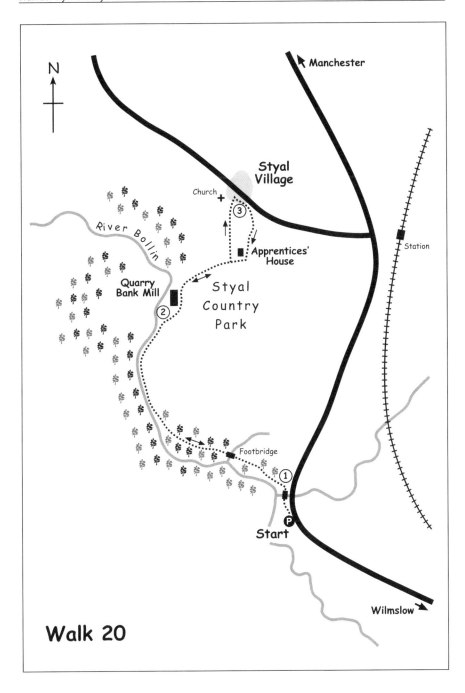

Walk 20

this stone. Turn left at a junction, along a path between the mill pond on the right and the river. Cross a little wooden bridge.

2. Turn left at a junction, pass a playground for young children and go through a gate to reach the mill building, with shop and café. The shorter walk ends here. For the longer walk continue past the mill, along the access road, steadily uphill for some distance. Approach the Apprentice House, but turn left at a sign 'Styal Village' 50m before the House. Follow the path beside a fence, go through a gate, then across a meadow to another gate. Cross a lane to yet another gate and reach the village. The Norcliffe Unitarian Chapel, built by the Greg family, is a short distance to the left, under the Lych Gate; the base of the ancient Styal Cross is on the right.

3. To return (without going into the village), bear right past the cross and take the first track on the right, passing more houses and the Methodist Church. Go through a gate 'no vehicles' and follow the broad roadway between hedges. Reach the Apprentice House, on the right, Turn right to pass the House and rejoin the mill access road, descending to return to the car park by the same route.

Walk 21: Alderley Edge

Assessment: Grade 1.

A small amount of ascent is the only relevant factor in this delightfully easy walk.

Distance: 1.5km (1 mile).

Total ascent: 25m (82ft).

Start/car parking: Large National Trust pay and display car park with public conveniences and picnic area at the Wizard restaurant/tea room, on the road linking Alderley Edge and Macclesfield, B5087, grid reference 860772.

Refreshments: Wizard tea room.

Map: Ordnance Survey Explorer 268, Wilmslow, Macclesfield and Congleton, 1:25,000.

The Area

Alderley Edge is a remarkable country area, barely escaping the outer fringe of the Manchester conurbation. The 'Edge', a sandstone ridge high above the adjacent plain, has a long history of mining activity. The Romans continued the extraction of copper ore already commenced by their Bronze Age predecessors; unsurprisingly, the Edge is honeycombed with pits and tunnels. At one time treeless, a sandy heathland, the Edge became part of a stately estate in 1602. Re-planting followed over the years, with the addition of picturesque follies such as the 'Druid's Stone Circle'. The mining rights were sold by the estate owners. From the 19th century limited public access was allowed; purchase by the National Trust in 1948 extended this access. Many previously dangerous mine entrances were made safe.

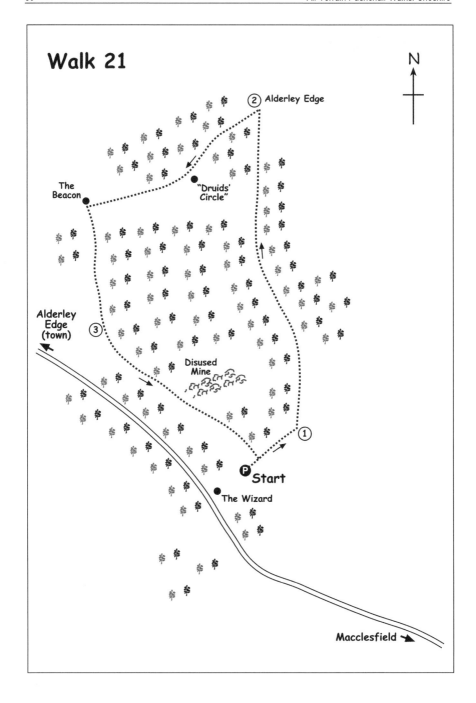

Walk 21

N

② Alderley Edge

The
Beacon

"Druids'
Circle"

Alderley
Edge
(town)

③

Disused
Mine

①

ⓟ Start

The Wizard

Macclesfield ➤

Alderley Edge

The Walk

From the tea shop set off along the 'Carriage Road', a broad roadway, with a meadow to the right. Ignore a path on the left.

1. Turn left through a gate into woodland, following a broad earth track through the trees, rising to reach Stormy Point, a marvellous viewpoint at the top of an expanse of sandstone rock and boulders.

2. Turn sharp left to descend gently along a broad track past the 'Druid's Stone Circle', soon reaching the site of the Armada Beacon on its little knoll. Before the Beacon, the track rakes back to the left. To the right is the corner of a stone wall. Ignore a right fork and continue to a crossing of tracks.

3. Go straight across (arrows on post), pass a fenced-off area on the left which is the site of much mining activity which includes the Engine Vein and a Roman shaft. A little side path facilitates viewing. Continue downhill to return to the tea room and car park.

Walk 22: Lyme Park

Assessment: *Grade 2.*

No impediments and good surfaces, but a prolonged ascent.

Distance: 5.3km (3¼ miles).

Total ascent: 92m (302ft).

Start/car parking: Parking area by the roadside on Shrigley Road, between Pott Shrigley and Higher Poynton, approximately 150m north of Pott Shrigley Methodist Chapel, grid reference 949817.

Refreshments: Café at Lyme Hall.

Map: Ordnance Survey Explorer 268, Wilmslow, Macclesfield and Congleton, 1:25,000 or Explorer OL1, the Peak District, Dark Peak area, 1:25,000.

The Area

Lyme Park covers a great swathe of moorland on the fringe of the Peak District. Lyme Hall is a stately home, managed by the National Trust as a major visitor attraction, with the usual catering and shop facilities. The park is noted for its herds of deer and is crossed by many walking routes, including the Gritstone Trail.

The Walk

Walk up the road, quite steeply, to the Methodist Chapel.

1. Turn sharp left along a surfaced roadway, as far as West Lodge. Turn right at the Lodge, in front of the house, to a gate with a 'National Trust, Lyme Park' sign. The roadway, West Park Drive, now ascends steadily by the side of a valley-bottom stream for more than half a mile, as far as a car park. Rhododendrons and bluebells are in profusion. Ignore any tracks to left or right. Go through a gate into the car park and continue along the tarmac road to the main car park and the Hall.

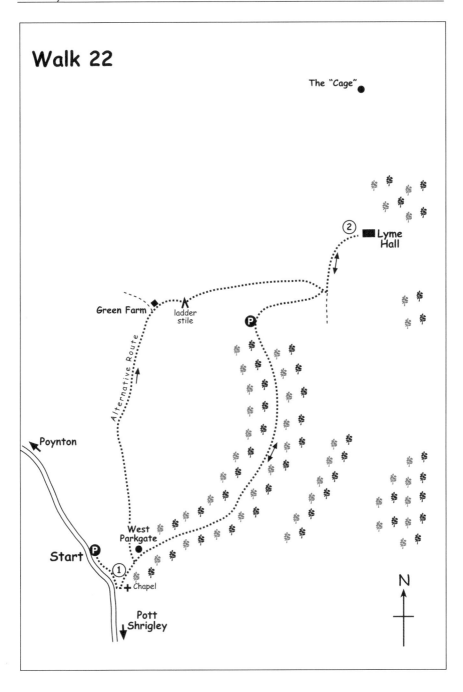

Walk 22

The "Cage"

② Lyme Hall

Green Farm — ladder stile

P

Alternative Route

Poynton

West Parkgate

Start P ①

+ Chapel

Pott Shrigley

N

Lyme Hall

2.   Return by the same route.

To avoid using the same route twice: it is possible to use a variation, preferably on the outward portion:

Do not turn right at West Lodge. Continue to rise on the roadway, passing the entrance to West Park Gate Farm before bearing left over a cattle grid and rising less steeply across the hillside, with extensive views to the left. Approach Green Farm and a junction of tracks, turning right to pass the farm buildings, then right again along a waymarked narrow path. There is a gate and a ladder stile, which must be passed to enter Lyme Park.

After the stile follow a rising grass track. The house 'Four Winds' is below to the left. Join a rough stone-surfaced track, going ahead, slightly downhill. At a 'T' junction turn left, now on tarmac, to descend to the main car park and the Hall.

Return by reversing the recommended outward route.

Walk 23: Higher Poynton (Middlewood Way)

Assessment: Grade I

A very easy walk combining part of the designated Middlewood Way with the towpath of the Macclesfield Canal, ensuring predominantly level walking with good surfaces underfoot. No stiles or steps.

Distance: 4.3km (2¾ miles).

Total ascent: Negligible.

Start/car parking: By the canal marina at Higher Poynton, with visitor centre and Lyme View restaurant, grid reference 945834.

Refreshments: Miners' Arms and Boar's Head Inns.

Map: Ordnance Survey Explorer OL1, The Peak District, Dark Peak area, 1:25,000.

The Area

This walk passes through a pleasantly rural area along the eastern extremity of the Cheshire Plain, with the Peak District foothills adjacent.

The Macclesfield Canal, 26 miles long, was opened in 1831, late in the canal age, connecting the Peak Forest Canal at Marple with the Trent and Mersey Canal at Hall Green, providing a direct route for narrow boats between the Potteries and Manchester The engineer was the great Thomas Telford. It shortened the distance from Manchester to London by 13 miles. The canal now forms part of the 'Cheshire Ring' of navigable waterways. The most important use of the canal was in transporting coal from Poynton collieries, silk from Macclesfield, cotton from Bollington and gritstone from Kerridge

The construction of the railway from Marple to Macclesfield was the result of the desire of the North Staffordshire Railway Company to have a direct route to Manchester. This was in partnership with

The Macclesfield canal

the Manchester Sheffield and Lincolnshire Railway (later part of the Great Central), thus avoiding use of the tracks of the rival London and North Western Railway. Before the construction was completed in 1869, however, a deal with the LNWR made the through route no longer necessary and, for passengers, the line became nothing more than a minor part of the Manchester suburban services based on what was then Manchester London Road station. However, from 1872 until closure of the Poynton collieries in 1935, a great deal of coal was carried. The line was closed to all traffic in 1970, being opened as the Middlewood Way for horse riders, cyclists and walkers in 1985.

The Walk

Set off through the wide gates, along the tarmac roadway to the higher part of the car park. Ahead are a few steps. Avoid these by diverting a few metres to the left to pass through a generous kissing gate, reaching the marina.

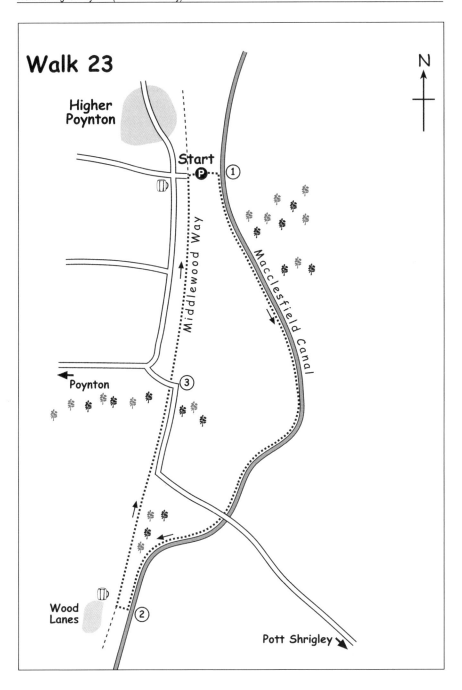

Walk 23

Higher Poynton

Start

Middlewood Way

Macclesfield Canal

Poynton

Wood Lanes

Pott Shrigley

N

1. Turn right to continue along the canal-side towpath. There is a
    hut selling refreshments, maps and gifts. Rise over a bridge
    spanning an arm of the canal. Water fowl and moored boats,
    many of them in the traditional narrow boat form, are plentiful.
    Leave the marina under bridge no.15. There are more moored
    boats as the canal contours along the lower slops of the western
    extremity of the Peak District hills, with the edge of the Cheshire
    Plain below to the right. Pass under the lattice-sided bridge
    no.16, then bridge no.17, then pass Ram's Clough Cottage,
    before reaching another large marina. The ubiquitous mallard
    are much in evidence.

2. Leave the canal immediately before bridge no.18. Go through a
    kissing gate to join the public highway. Turn right, gently down-
    hill, passing the Lyme View Restaurant on the right. In 50m turn
    right at a kissing gate signposted 'Middlewood Way'. The
    Miners' Arms Inn is a short distance further along the road.
    Continue along a good track, for some distance staying above the
    former railway trackbed at the bottom of the cutting. Descend
    gently to join the trackbed by bridge no.13. A low fence sepa-
    rates the tracks approved for horses, cycles and pedestrians. The
    Way is almost level as it passes through mixed woodland, with
    abundant conifers.

3. Reach a small parking area and continue; there are information
    boards by the entrance to Poynton Coppice, offering a woodland
    walk – but not apparently for ATPs as the path is narrow, with
    steps. The track rises, passing under bridge no.14. The former
    Higher Poynton station is soon reached. Bear left, along the plat-
    form. There are picnic tables and a plaque recording the open-
    ing of the Middlewood Way by David Ballamy on 30th May,
    1985. At the far end of the platform rise up a cobbled ramp.
    There is a 'Nelson Pit Visitor Centre, Canal, Café, Pub.' signpost.
    Go through a kissing gate to join the public highway opposite
    the Boar's Head Inn. Turn right, then right again to cross the
    bridge over the Middlewood Way before turning left into the car
    park.

Walk 24: Bollington

Assessment: *Grade 2.*

An easy walk, making use of the Middlewood Way and the towpath of the Macclesfield Canal to provide a good, level, route on good surfaces, without stiles or other impediments. Grade 2 only because of the descent of a flight of steps at the start of the walk.

Distance: 4km (2½ miles).

Total ascent: Negligible.

Start/car parking: Public car park, Holehouse Lane, grid reference 927790, accessed from the A523 north of Macclesfield, through Whiteley Green. The distance from main road to car park is less than 1½ miles. Alternatively, approached from Bollington the car park is a little more than one mile to the north, along Adlington Road and Sugar House Lane,

Refreshments: The Windmill Inn is 200m from the start of the walk.

Map: Ordnance Survey Explorer 268, Wilmslow, Macclesfield and Congleton, 1:25,000.

The Area

Bollington is a small former mill (cotton) town to the north of Macclesfield situated at the point where the Cheshire Plain meets the foothills of the Peak District. The Macclesfield Canal provided transport for materials to and from several of the town's mills. For information on the canal and the former railway, see walk 23.

The Walk

From the entrance to the car park, walk along the public highway, crossing the bridge over the Middlewood Way in 50m.

Turn left immediately to descend a slightly awkward flight of steps before reaching the track bed of the former railway line.

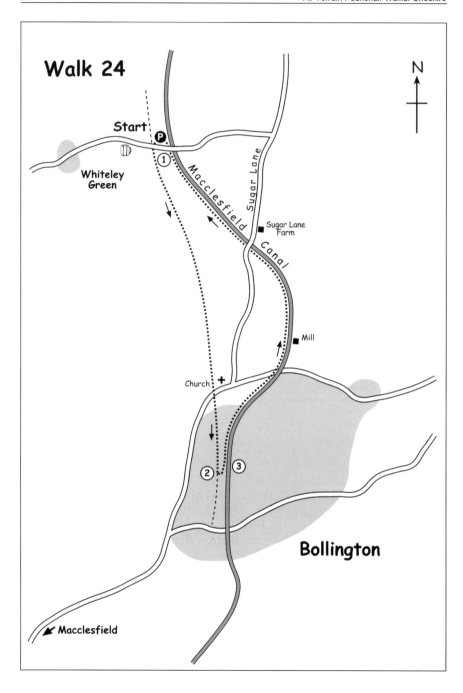

Walk 24

N

Start

Whiteley
Green

Macclesfield

Sugar Lane

Sugar Lane
Farm

Canal

Mill

Church

Bollington

Macclesfield

Canal bridge near Bollington

1. Turn right to continue along the level Way, approved for horses, cycles and pedestrians, largely in a cutting. There is a parallel path above to the left, but the trackbed is preferable for ATPs. Pass a sculpture in wood. The spire of a church at the north end of Bollington comes into view as a substantial viaduct is approached. Pass a sign giving distances to Marple and to Macclesfield. The opening to the viaduct is tight; ATPs are probably bettered pushed under a barrier 50m before reaching the viaduct. There is a ramp here down to the Adlington Road car park. Cross the viaduct, with a bird's eye view of much of Bollington below. Pass Bollington Arts Centre and the church with the spire already seen from a distance. The trackbed now rises steadily, passing under a road bridge.

2. Turn sharp right to rake back up a ramp to reach a very minor road, through a narrow opening at the top. Turn right, rising along an unsurfaced lane to reach the canal in 100m. Go through a gate to access the towpath.

3.   Turn left to follow the towpath, passing moored boats and houses on the fringe of Bollington. There are plenty of mallard on the water and occasional seats along the towpath. Go under bridge 27; note the slots provided for 'stop boards' to seal off sections of the canal when maintenance works are carried out. Pass Aqueduct Cottage on the left, cross over the aqueduct to reach the fine Clarence Mill, built at about the same time as the canal was constructed. There is a useful information board. The mill relied heavily on the canal for supplies of raw cotton and of coal for its steam engines. After closure in the late1960s the mill was converted into small industrial/commercial units. Pass under bridge 26, again with provision for stop boards, the canal now in pleasantly rural surroundings. Pass under bridge 25, turning at once into the car park.

Walk 25: Tegg's Nose Country Park

Assessment: Grade 2.

Some rise and fall but all surfaces are good and there are no gates or stiles.

Distance: 3km (2 miles).

Total ascent: 35m (115ft).

Start/car parking: Pay and display car park at the Tegg's Nose visitor centre, grid reference 950733. From Macclesfield accessed by the Old Buxton Road.

Refreshments: None.

Map: Ordnance Survey Explorer 268, Wilmslow, Macclesfield and Congleton, 1:25,000.

The Area

This is a superb part of Cheshire, high in the rolling hills of Macclesfield Forest, part of the Peak District. Tegg's Nose provided large quantities of stone for more than four centuries until closure in 1995; some of the quarry machinery has been preserved on site. The well-equipped visitor centre has picnic tables, public conveniences and great views over the surrounding countryside, including the reservoirs which supply water to Macclesfield,

This most enjoyable short walk is a circuit close to the top of the 'Nose', with an optional diversion to the top.

The Walk

Leave the visitor centre by the vehicular access. Turn left at once along an inviting wide track signposted 'to the country park', rising gently to a gate. Macclesfield is in view. At the next gate ignore steps to the left.

1. In a further 40m turn left at a yellow waymark, rising. Stay with the main track at a junction, still rising, now among the former quarries, richly carpeted with heather and bilberry. Just below

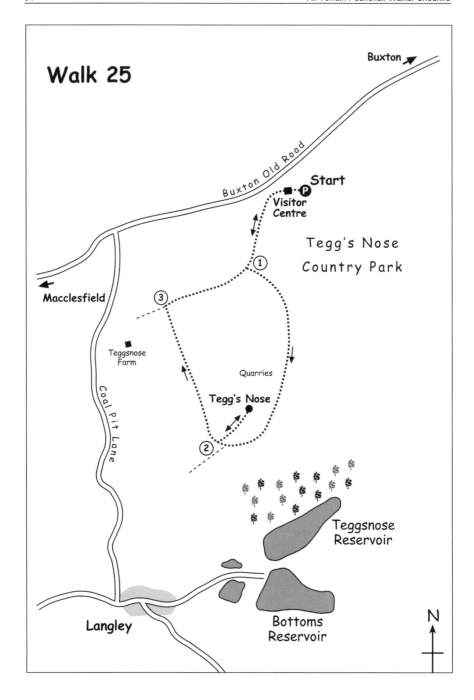

Walk 25

Buxton

Buxton Old Road

Start

Visitor
Centre

Tegg's Nose
Country Park

①

Macclesfield

③

Teggsnose
Farm

Quarries

Coal Pit Lane

Tegg's Nose

②

Teggsnose
Reservoir

Langley

Bottoms
Reservoir

N

Quarry machinery, Tegg's Nose Country Park

the top of the hill there are exposed quarry faces. Pass an information board and preserved items of quarry machinery.

Pass a 'Tegg's Nose sign and a waymark and go straight ahead at a fork. Pass a seat at a fine viewpoint. As the track becomes rougher, ignore paths to left and right. The village of Langley and two small reservoirs are in view below. Bear round to the right and ignore a left turn which takes the Tegg's Nose Trail down to the left, through a gate. Rise gently to a gate.

2. From the gate, to continue the circuit turn left, downhill, over tarmac. To divert to the summit, go right, uphill, turn left in 60m along a narrow path, before a gate, rising to the summit in a short distance. There is a seat and a viewing table. Return by the same route to resume the circuit. There is plenty of gorse before a modern kissing gate is reached.

3. At a 'T' junction turn right, through another modern kissing gate, with a 'car park' sign, now on a track along the edge of a field. Go through a gate to rejoin the outward route and return to the car park.

Walk 26: Macclesfield Forest

Assessment: *Grade 5.*

Not particularly long, but quite a hard walk with considerable ascent. Some steps and potentially awkward kissing gates.

Distance: 5.5km (3½ miles).

Total ascent: 150m (492ft).

Start/car parking: Pay and display car park at Macclesfield Forest visitor centre, with public conveniences and picnic tables, grid reference 961711, accessed by a minor road from Langley village, passing along the side of Ridgegate Reservoir.

Refreshments: None (picnic area).

Map: Ordnance Survey Explorer OL24, The Peak District, White Peak area, 1:25,000.

The Area

Beautifully situated on the fringe of the Peak District, Macclesfield Forest has long been esteemed as an area for country walking. Reservoirs supplying Macclesfield add to the attraction of this visitor-friendly area of upland forest and wide open spaces, rich in wild life. There are several designated trails, including the Gritstone Trail and the Tegg's Nose Trail.

The Walk

Leave the visitor centre by the access roadway, turning right immediately before reaching the road to follow a track through the trees. A signpost mentions 'forest walks 1, 2, and 3'. This walk is basically no.2. The reservoir is in view. Go through a squeezer stile, then immediately to the right, along a broad unsurfaced roadway, rising steadily. At a junction stay with the main track, soon rising again. There is a 'Shutlingsloe' signpost.

The Visitor Centre *(Photograph: Graham Beech)*

1. At the next junction bear left with the main track '1, 2, 3' on a post. There are now pine trees to the right. At a signpost before a gate turn right for '2, Shutlingsloe', uphill. Pass a seat, rising more gently to a locked gate and an inadequate kissing gate. At a junction bear left with the main track; at a signpost 'standing stone 2, 3' go straight ahead. Pass a picnic table on the right and a 'standing stone' signpost, then a well-placed seat with views of the reservoir and Tegg's Nose. Descend briefly, pass an abandoned farm building and resume the ascent. The next section is almost level, with long views of high moorland, the Buxton road and the well-known Cat and Fiddle Inn. Pass a tiny pond on the left and a '2,3' signpost before reaching the public road at a gate.

2. Turn left before the gate to an inadequate kissing gate (the bank by the roadside might provide a better route) and continue along a narrow path parallel with the road, downhill. Go through a gate, then through a tight kissing gate to join the road. Cross over to a gate opposite. With an ATP it is probably better to walk down the road as far as a second little gate on the right. Go

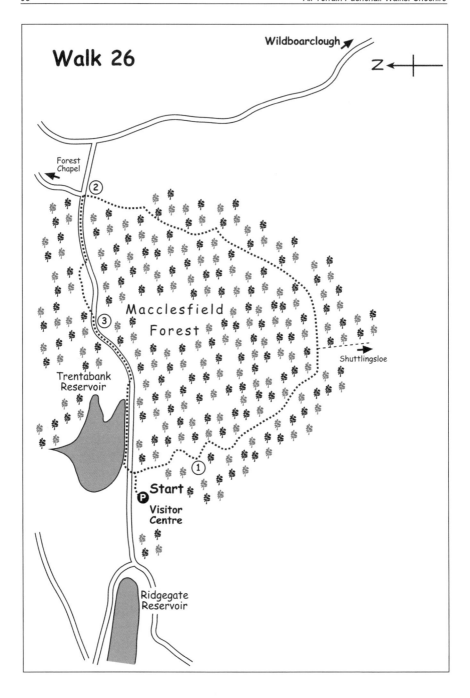

through this then, in a short distance, turn left along a minor path and cross a little bridge. The path soon widens, staying roughly parallel with the road. Reach a locked gate and go down steps to the left to join the road.

3.   Route no.2 goes through a narrow gap in the wall opposite; with an ATP most will prefer to walk along the side of the quiet road. Trentabank reservoir comes into view, with a parking lay-by and an information board concerning the famous heronry at the end of the reservoir. At the far end of the lay-by go through a gate to follow the roadside path. As the path goes to the right, turn left through a gate to the road, cross over and follow the 'easy access path' back to the visitor centre.

Walk 27: Congleton – Biddulph Way

Assessment: *Grade 4 (shorter version, Grade 3).*

A fair amount of ascent, steps and an awkward barrier.

Distance: 5.3km (3¼ miles). (Shorter version, 3km – 2 miles).

Total ascent: 40m (131ft). (Shorter version 15m – 49ft).

Start/car parking: Parking area at Congleton railway station, on the fringe of the town, accessed from Congleton via the Biddulph road, grid reference 872624. Note that the car park may well be full of commuters' cars on a weekday; you may find a space across the main road in one of the side-roads – or you could arrive by train!

Refreshments: None.

Map: Ordnance Survey Explorer 268, Wilmslow, Macclesfield and Congleton, 1:25,000.

The Area

This circuit combines part of the Biddulph Way (a former railway line), the towpath of the Macclesfield Canal and a bridleway to make a remarkably attractive route on the fringe of Congleton. Although the town has some good features it is, on the whole, not among the prettiest of Cheshire towns.

The Biddulph Way is one of the best of the former railway lines which have become trails. Heading into Congleton on a high embankment, the extensive views include the hill 'The Cloud'.

The Walk

From the station car park there is a choice. Either:

a) Go direct to the canal: from the station platform cross the railway line on the footbridge – up and down steps. At the far side of the tracks, turn right then in 30m turn left down a flight of steps, not in very good condition, direct to the towpath.

Approaching Bridge 74   *(Photograph: Graham Beech)*

Or,

b) To avoid the footbridge over the railway, walk back up the station approach road and turn sharp left along the roadside pavement, crossing over railway and canal. At the far end of the bridge cross the main road and then turn sharp right to walk back along a cul-de-sac road, passing the Railway Inn before turning right, under the road, to reach the same steps as in a). In either case, at the foot of the steps turn left to follow the towpath in pleasant surroundings through the fringe of residential Congleton. Pass under bridge 74, followed by bridge 73. The hill 'The Cloud' is in view as the canal passes over a great embankment; to the left is a fine railway viaduct.

Note: *In mid-August 2007, access to the flight of steps (referred to above) was closed by British Waterways, presumably to enable repairs to be made. Until these are completed it is suggested that walkers initially follow option (b) but, rather than crossing the main road, continue a little further and turn left into Morley Drive. Cross over the canal and, before the John Morley Industrial Unit, take the steps on your right down to the canal at bridge 74 and turn left.*

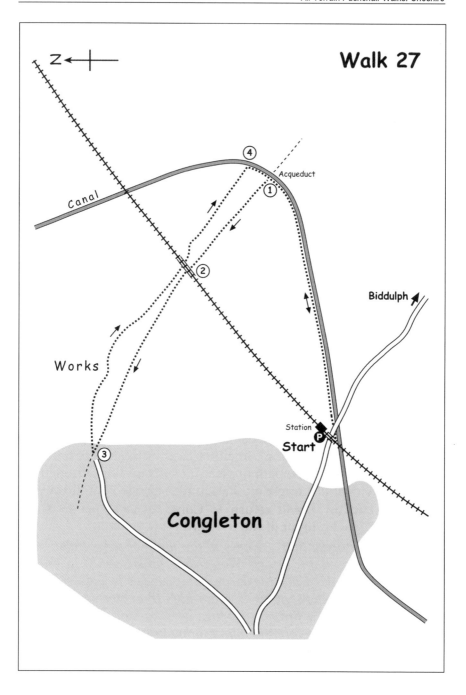

Walk 27

Canal

Acqueduct

① ②

④

Works

③

Biddulph

Station
Start

Congleton

1. At the far end of the embankment turn left, immediately before the canal passes over the former railway line. The barrier here has an awkward vertical post. Descend by an earth track and easy steps to the former trackbed. There is a 'Biddulph Way' information board. The trail has a good surface as it passes through well wooded surroundings, with abundant silver birch. Pass under a three-arch railway bridge – carrying the main line of the former North Staffordshire Railway.

2. For the short walk turn sharp right here. For the full circuit continue along the railway trail, passing squeezer stiles, each with a stepped access for horses beside. Go under another bridge, the track soon on embankments. After a little more than half a mile reach a stone bridge with a brick parapet.

3. Go up a fairly steep ramp on the left; there are cycle route signs. Go through a squeezer/horse access at the top of the ramp and turn sharp right to follow a road descending to cross a bridge over a rushing stream. Pass an industrial site and a terrace of houses. The roadway now rises steadily for some distance. Pass a track to Vale Cottage before reaching the high railway bridge at point 2. Pass a little terrace of houses and a pond on the left. Go under another bridge which carried a long defunct spur connecting the two railway lines. The track rises gently before reaching bridge 72 over the canal.

4. Turn right here, through a little gate, and go down a few easy steps to the towpath. Cross high over the Biddulph Way to outward point 1 and return to Congleton station along the towpath, using either of the outward route choices to return to the car park.

Walk 28: Brereton Heath

Assessment: Grade 1.

A short level walk with no impediments

Distance: 1.5km (1 mile).

Total ascent: Negligible.

Start/car parking: At Brereton Heath Visitor Centre, pay and display. About a quarter of a mile south of the A54 between Congleton and Holmes Chapel, signposted, grid reference 654795.

Refreshments: Picnic area only.

Map: Ordnance Survey Explorer 268, Wilmslow, Macclesfield and Congleton, 1:25,000.

The Area

Since 1982 Brereton Heath has been a small but attractive country park, having extra status as a local nature reserve added in 2004. The country park was originally a comparatively rare area of lowland heath, largely the grounds of the now demolished Brereton Hall. For thirteen years from 1959, there was large scale extraction of sand. Oak, rowan, hazel and others have supplemented the silver birch and pine trees in recent years, adding to the diversity of the wildlife habitat. The park is noted for Brimstone Yellow butterflies. The lake resulting from the sand extraction is popular for canoeing and angling.

The visitor centre has information and public conveniences.

The Walk

Start along the excellent, wheelchair-friendly track, heading away from the visitor centre, basically the 'Brimstone Trail'. Go straight ahead at the first junction, with a 'Brimstone Trail' signpost, entering mature woodland. Cross a bridge over a tiny, sluggish, stream. Pass a seat. As the track forks, bear left, passing a wood sculpture

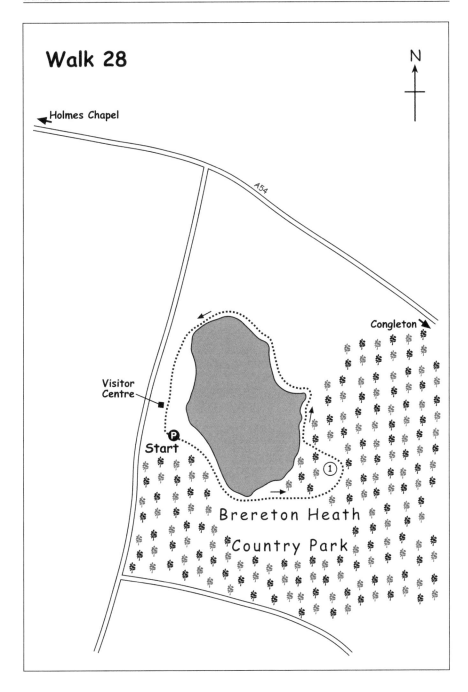

Local residents at Brereton Heath *(Photograph: Graham Beech)*

and a yellow marker. Cross another little bridge, reaching another fork.

1. Turn left, signposted 'lake' to join a broader track by the side of the lake in a few metres. Turn right to continue along this delightful track close to the lake. There is a 'Brimstone Trail' signpost. Stay with the track as it bends to the left. There are arches constructed from willow branches and picnic tables. Continue to bear left towards the visitor centre before returning to the car park.

Walk 29: Brereton Heath and Swettenham

Assessment: *Grade 3.*

There are no impediments or difficult surfaces but considerable rises, up each side of the Dane Valley.

Distance: 5.3km (3¼ miles).

Total ascent: 60m (197ft).

Start/car parking: Pay and display at the Visitor Centre, Brereton Heath Country Park (as in walk no. 28).

Refreshments: Inn at Swettenham

Map: Ordnance Survey Explorer 268, Wilmslow, Macclesfield and Congleton, 1:25,000.

The Area

Brereton Heath Country Park is described in walk no. 28.

Swettenham is a small but attractive village, enhanced by having only limited road access. At its heart are a church and a large, popular, inn.

The out-and-back route crosses the lovely valley of the River Dane. At the Brereton Heath end, there is 400m of walking by the side of a quiet minor road. More than a third of this roadside can be avoided by starting along the track to the north from the visitor centre, forking left after 150mto join the road, over a low stile.

The Walk

Leave the visitor centre by the vehicular access (or as suggested above), turning right to walk along the side of the minor road.

1. Cross the main A54 road, continuing down the tarmac-surfaced lane opposite. There are bridleway and 'Dane Valley Way' signs

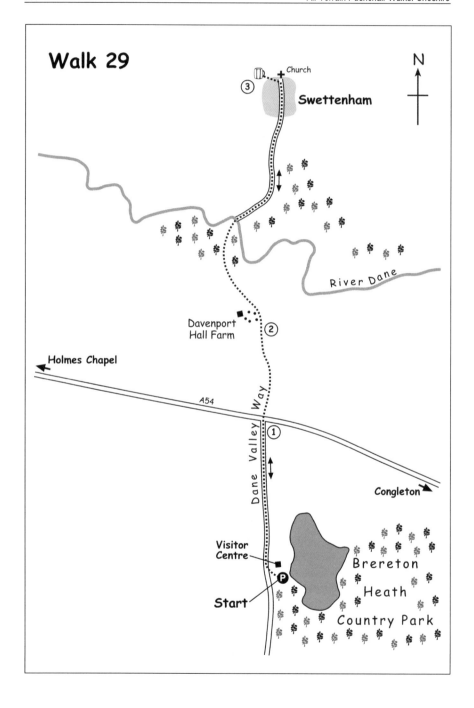

The Swettenham Arms – for a pub lunch or afternoon tea   *(Photograph: Graham Beech)*

on a post. Pass several large houses before reaching the gates of Davenport Hall. Go through, noting the instructions, now along a gravel surfaced track, the access to the Hall. There is an avenue of ornamental cherry trees.

2.   At a fork with a pond on the left keep right, then right again at the next fork, passing more ponds, now on the right. There is a gentle descent towards the Dane Valley on a fine track, with banks of bluebells in Spring. The descent continues to a waymarked gate and a bridge across the River Dane. There is a similar gate beside a house, then a steady rise up a surfaced roadway. As the road levels, pass the entrance to Swettenham cemetery on the right and enter the village. Reach the stone church with brick tower and turn left to the inn.

3.   Return by the same route.

The previous walk at Brereton Heath (walk no.28) can be joined to this walk if a longer route is desired.

Walk 30: Wheelock and the Trent and Mersey Canal

Assessment: Grade 1.

A short, almost level, route with one easy ramp.

Distance: 3km (2 miles).

Total ascent: 15m (49ft).

Start/car parking: By the side of the canal; turn off the main road through Wheelock at the Cheshire Cheese Inn, grid reference 751592.

Refreshments: Cheshire Cheese Inn, Wheelock.

Map: Ordnance Survey Explorer 268, Wilmslow, Macclesfield and Congleton, 1:25,000.

The Area

Although it is an old settlement in its own right, Wheelock now has the appearance of a southerly extension of Sandbach. There are a few old properties, one or two shops and the Cheshire Cheese Inn, pleasant enough but undistinguished.

There was a salt industry locally at Rode Heath; the former railway line carried coal and limestone from a junction with the main Crewe to Manchester line at Sandbach. There was also a passenger service. Since closure the line has become the Wheelock Rail Trail, an attractive route for walkers, cyclists and horse-riders and a wildlife haven noted for the diversity of wild flowers.

The Trent and Mersey was an early 'narrow' canal, part of the great engineer James Brindley's ambitious concept of a huge cross, linking the country's principal manufacturing areas. This canal joined the two great rivers and was very busy for many years, as evidenced by the double locks, with the potteries around Stoke on Trent providing a large part of the trade.

Combining canal and former railway line provides an interesting short walk.

Walk 30

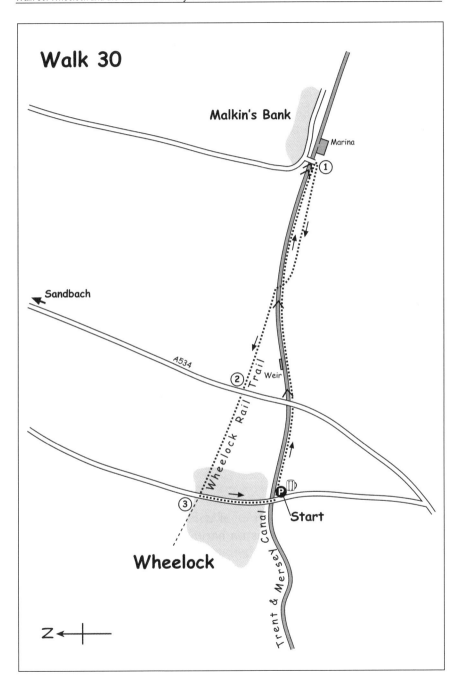

Malkin's Bank

Marina

①

Sandbach

A534

② Weir

Wheelock Rail Trail

P

Start

③

Wheelock

Trent & Mersey Canal

N

The Walk

Head away from the road along the canal towpath, passing a Trent and Mersey Canal information board. Go through a wide gate, over a stream and under a bridge carrying a main road to reach a double lock. There are traditional 'horse' cobbles still in situ beside the lock and a lock-keeper's cottage on the far bank. Continue past another double lock, passing a widened section of canal, for turning boats. Pass under a former railway bridge and keep to the towpath. There are more double locks and a bridge as the residential area of Malkin's Bank is reached, with cottages and a small marina.

The Trent and Mersey Canal at Wheelock

1. Return along the towpath for 40m then go left through a gap in the hedge to an excellent track which stays close to the canal, but is separated by a high hedge. On the left is a golf course and the views are quite different from those on the outward route. Bear right to rejoin the towpath but then go left immediately to walk uphill to the starting point of the Wheelock Rail Trail, along the trackbed of the former line. Go through a squeezer or gate to cross the bridge over the canal; there is an information

board. The Trail is well surfaced, largely on embankment, good for views.

2. Go through a little gate/squeezer and cross a main road to a similar gate/squeezer on the far side. Continue towards Wheelock, soon reaching the site of the former Wheelock station. Walk along the platform, pass an information board and rise up a ramp, passing the former station building before joining the road through Wheelock.

3. Turn left to follow the broad roadside footpath for about 300m back to the Cheshire Cheese Inn and the car parking area.

Also from Sigma Leisure:

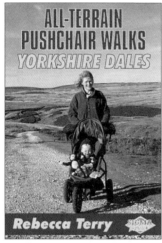

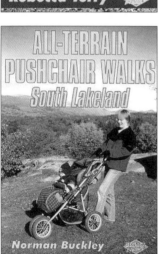

Other titles in our
"All-Terrain Pushchair Walks" series
include:

Anglesey & Lleyn Peninsula

North Lakeland

South Lakeland

North York Moors

Peak District

Snowdonia

West Yorkshire

Yorkshire Dales

All £7.95 each

All of our books are available through booksellers and Amazon.co.uk. For a free catalogue, contact:
SIGMA LEISURE, 5 ALTON ROAD, WILMSLOW, CHESHIRE SK9 5DY
Tel/Fax: 01625-531035   E-mail: info@sigmapress.co.uk
Web site: www.sigmapress.co.uk